GREAT BATTLES THROUGH THE AGES

BATTLE OF THE BULGE

KOREA 1950:
PUSAN TO CHOSIN

THE THIRD CRUSADE:
RICHARD THE LIONHEARTED vs. SALADIN

SINKING OF THE *BISMARCK*

THE *MONITOR* vs. THE *MERRIMACK*

BATTLE OF ACTIUM

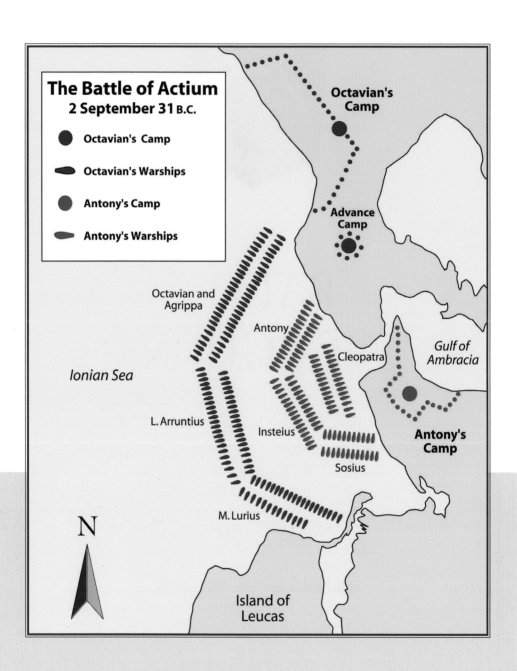

The Battle of Actium
2 September 31 B.C.

- ⬤ Octavian's Camp
- ▬ Octavian's Warships
- ⬤ Antony's Camp
- ▬ Antony's Warships

Octavian's
Camp

Advance
Camp

Gulf of
Ambracia

Octavian and
Agrippa

Antony

Cleopatra

Ionian Sea

L. Arruntius

Insteius

Antony's
Camp

Sosius

M. Lurius

N

Island of
Leucas

BATTLE
OF ACTIUM

DAVID J. CALIFF

INTRODUCTION BY
CASPAR W. WEINBERGER

CHELSEA HOUSE
PUBLISHERS

A Haights Cross Communications Company

Philadelphia

FRONTIS: Map of the Battle of Actium

CHELSEA HOUSE PUBLISHERS

VP, PRODUCT DEVELOPMENT Sally Cheney
DIRECTOR OF PRODUCTION Kim Shinners
CREATIVE MANAGER Takeshi Takahashi
MANUFACTURING MANAGER Diann Grasse

STAFF FOR BATTLE OF ACTIUM

EXECUTIVE EDITOR Lee Marcott
PRODUCTION ASSISTANT Megan Emery
PICTURE RESEARCHER Sarah Bloom
SERIES & COVER DESIGNER Keith Trego
LAYOUT 21st Century Publishing and Communications, Inc.

A Haights Cross Communications ✦ Company

http://www.chelseahouse.com

First Printing

1 3 5 7 9 8 6 4 2

Library of Congress Cataloging-in-Publication Data

Califf, David J.
  Battle of Actium / by David J. Califf.
    p. cm.—(Great battles through the ages)
Summary: Recounts events leading up to and surrounding the 31 B.C.
Battle of Actium during the Roman Civil War, as well as its long-lasting
consequences. Includes bibliographical references and index.
  ISBN 0-7910-7440-4 (hardcover)
  1. Rome—History—Civil War, 43-31 B.C—Juvenile literature.
2. Actium, Battle of, 31 B.C.—Juvenile literature. [1. Rome—History—
Civil War, 43-31 B.C. 2. Actium, Battle of, 31 B.C. 3. Naval battles.]
I. Title. II. Series.
DG268.C33 2003
937'.05—dc21
                                                2003009476

TABLE OF CONTENTS

INTRODUCTION BY CASPAR W. WEINBERGER   6

1 FROM THE ORIGINS OF ROME TO
    THE COLLAPSE OF THE REPUBLIC   11

2 THE SECOND TRIUMVIRATE   31

3 PHILIPPI   39

4 SEXTUS POMPEIUS   45

5 OCTAVIAN VERSUS ANTONY
    AND CLEOPATRA   55

6 ROMAN NAVAL WARFARE   63

7 THE ACTIAN CAMPAIGN   69

8 THE AGE OF AUGUSTUS   87

9 ACTIUM IN LITERATURE   99

CHRONOLOGY   108

NOTES   109

BIBLIOGRAPHY   110

INDEX   111

INTRODUCTION

by Caspar W. Weinberger

There are many ways to study and teach history, which has perhaps been best defined as the "recording and interpretation of past events." Concentration can be on a compilation of major events, or on those events that help prove a theory of the author's. Or the "great man" theory can be applied to write the history of a country or an era, based on a study of the principal leaders or accepted geniuses who are felt to have shaped events that became part of the tapestry of history.

This new Chelsea House series adopts and continues the plan of studying six of the major battles and turning points of wars that did indeed shape much of the history of the periods before, during, and after those wars. By studying the events leading up to major battles and their results, inescapably one learns a great deal about the history of that period.

The first battle, chosen appropriately enough, is the Battle of Actium. There, in 31 B.C., the naval forces of Antony and Cleopatra, and those of Octavian, did battle off the northwest coast of Greece for control of the Roman world. Octavian's victory ended the Roman civil war and gave him unchallenged supremacy, leading to his designation as Augustus, Rome's first emperor. It is highly appropriate that the Battle of Actium be studied first for this series, because the battle was for many decades used as the starting point for a new era.

Next, in chronological order, is a study of the long years of battles between the forces of Richard the Lionhearted and Saladin. This Third Crusade, during the twelfth century, and the various military struggles for Acre and Jerusalem, was the background against which much of the history of modern Britain and Europe and the Middle East was played out.

Coming down to modern times, the series includes a study of the battle that forever changed naval warfare. This battle, the first between two ironclad warships, the *Monitor* and the *Merrimack*, ended the era of naval wars fought by great fleets of sail- or oar-powered ships, with their highly intricate maneuvers. After the *Monitor* and *Merrimack*, all naval battles became floating artillery duels with wholly different tactics and skills required.

The sinking of the German ship *Bismarck* during World War II was not so much a battle as a clear demonstration of the fact that a huge preponderance of naval force on one side could hunt down and destroy one of the most powerful battleships then afloat.

The continued importance of infantry warfare was demonstrated in the Battle of the Bulge, the final attempt of the German army, near the end of World War II, to stave off what in hindsight is now seen as the inevitable victory of the Allies.

The last battle in this series covers the Korean War—one of the most difficult and costly we have fought, and yet a war whose full story is very nearly forgotten by historians and teachers. The story of the Korean War embodies far more than simply the history of a war we fought in the 1950s. It is a history that is dominated by General Douglas MacArthur— but it is also a history of many of the foundation stores of American foreign and domestic policy in the past half century.

These six battles, and the wars of which they were a part, are well worth studying because, although they obviously cannot recount all of history from Actium to Korea, they can and do show the reader the similarities of many of those issues that drive people and governments to war. They also recount the development and changes in technologies by which people have acquired the ability to destroy their fellow creatures ever more effectively and completely.

With the invention and deployment of each new instrument of destruction, from the catapults that were capable of blasting great holes in the walls defending castles and forts, to today's nuclear weapons, the prediction has always been made that the effects and capability of each of those engines of destruction were so awful that their very availability would end war entirely. Thus far, those predictions have always been wrong, although as the full potential of nuclear weapons of mass destruction is increasingly better understood, it may well be that the very nature of these ultimate weapons will, indeed, mean that they will ever be used. However, the sheer numbers of these ultimate weapons possessed by many countries, and the possibilities of some of those countries falling under the dictatorship of some of the world's most dangerous leaders, combine to make imaginable a war that could indeed end the world. That is why the United States has expended so much to try to prevent countries such as Iraq and North Korea from continuing to be led by men as inherently dangerous as Saddam Hussein and Kim Il Sung, who are determined to acquire the world's most dangerous weapons.

An increasing knowledge of some of the great battles of the past that have so influenced history is essential unless we want to fulfill the old adage that those who forget history are likely to be condemned to repeat it—with all of its mistakes.

This old adage reminds us also that history is a study not just of great military victories, but also the story of battles lost and the many mistakes that were made by even the greatest of commanders.

After every engagement that involves American troops in action, even on a very small scale, the Pentagon conducts a "Lessons Learned" exercise. What went wrong? What should have been done differently? Did we need more troops, more artillery, more planes? Most important, could more lives of our own troops have been saved?

These mistakes or command errors are not only carefully studied and written about, but they form the basis for war games or exercises in which actual battle situations are re-fought—sometimes on paper—but frequently with troops re-enacting various parts of the combat action. These "lessons learned" exercises become a valuable part of the training of troops and are an even more valuable part of the training of leaders and commanders.

As we can all guess from the short discussions of some of those great battles in this series, there were many opportunities for different commanders and different plans to be used. Indeed, history is perhaps our greatest teacher, and a study of great battles is a great way to learn, even though each battle is different and there will be different lessons to be learned from the post-battle studies.

So, this Chelsea House series serves as a splendid beginning to our study of military history—a history that we must master if we want to see the expansion and success of our basic policy of maintaining peace with freedom.

It is not enough to consider threats to our security and our freedom. We must also be constantly ready to defend our freedom by keeping our ability to prevent any of those threats against us from materializing into real dangers. The study of great battles and how they were won, despite mistakes that have been made, is a vital part of our ability to keep peace with freedom.

BY: Caspar W. Weinberger
Chairman, FORBES Inc.
March 2003

Caspar W. Weinberger was the fifteenth U.S. secretary of defense,
serving under President Ronald Reagan from 1981 to 1987.

From the
Origins of Rome
to the Collapse
of the Republic

Augustus and Cleopatra were two key figures—and adversaries—in the Battle of Actium. Cleopatra had known Augustus's great-uncle, Caesar, when Caesar traveled to Egypt to defeat Pompey about 48 B.C.

INTRODUCTION TO ACTIUM: THE STAKES

To students of Roman history, 31 B.C., the year of the Battle of Actium, is as familiar a date as 753 B.C., the year of the founding of Rome, or 509 B.C., the year of the establishment of the Roman Republic. On September 2 of that year, Gaius Julius Octavianus Caesar, the adoptive son of Julius Caesar and the man who would later be known as Augustus, defeated the forces of Marc Antony and Cleopatra in a naval battle just outside the Ambracian Gulf along the western coast of Greece. Octavian's victory at Actium achieved the final consolidation of unchallenged power in the hands of one man, marking the official end of republican government and the beginning of a principate that would endure for centuries.

By establishing this imperial government, Augustus brought about the end of the free state, but he also brought an end to the brutal civil wars that had gripped Rome for decades. Under his reign, Rome reaped the benefits of the *Pax Romana*, a period of unparalleled peace and prosperity and a flowering of the arts that rivaled the Golden Age of fifth-century Athens.

For these reasons, the Battle of Actium is justly considered to be an important moment in Roman, and world, history. Like most pivotal moments, however, Actium was not simply an abrupt and unexpected break with the past. It was also very much a product of the past and in some ways an extension of the more subtle yet no less decisive political changes that were taking place in Rome during the first century B.C. Furthermore, Actium must also be understood within the long arc of Roman history, for the battle and the events leading up to it lie within the broader context of themes, values, and patterns of events that had defined Roman civilization for centuries.

THE MYTHIC BEGINNINGS OF ROME

The story of Rome's foundation is one of legendary heroes and epic adventure. In Greco-Roman mythology, there was once a Golden Age in which the gods lived on Earth and provided an easy life for mortals. There was no war, no strife, no disease, and the untilled land brought forth food in abundance without any effort from humans. This Golden Age, however, did not last forever. It degenerated into a silver and then a bronze age, an age of heroes in which gods and people still interacted but an age that also knew war.

It is in this heroic "bronze age" that the mythic seeds

of Rome were sown. At a wedding banquet, the goddess of Discord, who, naturally enough, had not been invited, tossed a golden apple into the middle of the crowd. The apple was inscribed, "For the most beautiful one." No mortal woman would have dared to claim such a prize in the presence of divinities, but three goddesses each claimed ownership of the apple: Hera, queen of the gods; Athena, goddess of war and wisdom; and Aphrodite, goddess of love. A Trojan prince named Paris was chosen to decide the contest, and he judged Aphrodite to be the winner.

As a reward for his wise choice, Aphrodite promised that he could have the most beautiful mortal in the world—Helen, who was at the time already married to the Spartan King Menelaus. The precise manner of Helen's abduction is variously told by ancient sources, but Menelaus was understandably anxious to have his wife back, so he assembled a mighty army under the command of his brother, Agamemnon, and sailed to Troy in the hope of crushing the Trojans and bringing Helen home.

For ten years, the Greek forces tried to capture the city of Troy but could never successfully penetrate its defenses. In a stratagem devised by the crafty hero Odysseus, the Greeks pretended to give up the fight and sail home. They built a large, wooden horse, ostensibly as an offering to their patron goddess Athena, but in reality the horse was nothing more than a trick, for its belly held an entire battalion of soldiers. With the fleet safely hidden behind the neighboring island of Tenedos, a Greek spy named Sinon convinced the Trojans that his countrymen had sailed home and that the wooden horse would bring good fortune to Troy if it was moved within the city walls. The Trojans foolishly took his advice. Later that night, the soldiers descended from the horse, attacked the city from within, and opened the gates to the Greek army, which had sailed back from Tenedos. Troy was lost.

With the city in flames and its commanding general, Hector, slain by the Greek hero Achilles, there remained but one man who could lead the surviving Trojans to safety: Aeneas, the son of the goddess Aphrodite and a mortal named Anchises. Hector appeared to Aeneas in a dream and advised his friend to leave the city. As Aeneas would later learn, it was his destiny to sail to Italy and establish a new Troy that would one day defeat Greece and rule the world.

This story, though it has little historical basis, is nevertheless instructive for our understanding of the Battle of Actium. Octavian, like his great-uncle Julius Caesar, claimed to be a descendant of the hero Aeneas and, by extension, of the goddess Venus, the Roman Aphrodite. Furthermore, Octavian's chief rival, Marc Antony, had long associated himself with Greece. As a result, Octavian could cast the conflict in the kind of "Rome versus Greece" terms that would resonate politically, and it is no accident that he would later commission the poet Virgil to write an epic about Aeneas, in which the hero is told that his descendants will one day preside over a new "Golden Age."

Although Aeneas is associated with the beginnings of Rome, he did not actually found the city himself, nor did his son Ascanius, who founded the city of Alba Longa. There, the first descendants of Aeneas ruled for several centuries as the so-called "Alban Kings." One of these kings, Numitor, became involved in a power struggle with his brother Aemulius. Aemulius deposed Numitor, killed his brother's son, and made Numitor's daughter, Rhea Silvia, a Vestal Virgin. Because these priestesses of Vesta were not allowed to marry or have children, Aemulius felt confident that Numitor would

According to legend, the founding of Rome began with twins Romulus and Remus, sons of the mortal Rhea Silvia and Mars, a god. The twins were raised by a female wolf and eventually ruled the city.

have no heirs and that his own power would therefore be secure.

Rhea Silvia, however, became pregnant by the god Mars with the twin sons Romulus and Remus. Aemulius ordered the boys to be drowned in the Tiber River, but their cradle washed ashore on the Palatine Hill, in the heart of what would one day become Rome. There, they were nursed by a she-wolf.

When the boys grew up, they deposed Aemulius and restored Numitor to the throne. After Numitor's death, his grandchildren fought with each other, and Romulus eventually killed his brother Remus in order to become the leader of a new city, which he named Rome, after himself.

For several hundred years, Rome was ruled by kings, but some of them were ineffective leaders with tyrannical tendencies. The people of Rome eventually expelled the last of these kings, Tarquin the Proud, in 510 B.C. Within a year, they established a more democratic form of government to take the place of the monarchy.

THE ROMAN REPUBLIC

The Romans chose to organize themselves as a republic, a form of government based upon shared power among elected officials and a strong Senate with the authority to make laws. Each year, the people would elect two chief magistrates called consuls. The consuls served a one-year term, after which they could govern a province, serve in the Senate, assume a military command, or return to private life. Both consuls had to agree on all major policy decisions and had to function in cooperation with the Senate. This system may have been inefficient, but it was the direct outgrowth of the Romans' negative experiences with kingship.

For many centuries, the republican system worked very well. Schoolchildren were trained in rhetoric, the art of public speaking, and political awareness and participation came to be regarded as a normal part of responsible citizenship. A young man who wanted to embark on a political career (an option unavailable to women) might study law, much as today, or he might serve in the military.

His first elected office would be that of quaestor, a low-level financial officer. Although quaestors had no authority to set policy, they were responsible for managing tax collection, government payments, crop subsidies, imports and exports, and other related matters. By the first century B.C., a quaestor was also automatically eligible for membership in the Senate.

The office of aedile was the next step in the *cursus honorum*, the "honors race," or sequence of offices held by a politician aspiring to the consulship. Aediles were mid-level administrators who performed whatever duties the consuls assigned but whose chief responsibilities included managing public works projects and organizing games, festivals, and other public entertainments. While it was technically possible to skip the aedileship, few chose that option, for being an aedile enabled a politician to perform the kind of constituent service that would build support for future campaigns.

The highest officials below the consuls were called praetors. The praetors were responsible for administering the court system and often served as judges. In early Roman times, praetors were not judicial officials but rather military officers, and even at the height of the republic, many former praetors took up military commands before, or instead of, seeking the consulship. Indeed, since the minimum age for praetor was 30 and the minimum age for consul was 42, the ex-praetors often held high-level but nonelected government posts, principally in the provinces.

From the start, the Roman Republic faced internal conflicts. The Roman people were divided into two classes: the patricians (mostly large land owners) and the plebeians (mostly small farmers, tradesmen, and other laborers). At first, only patricians could serve in the Senate or elect consuls from their own number. The plebeians were represented by a popular assembly called the *Consilium Plebis*, with officers known as Tribunes of the People. Although this body did perform a legislative function, the patricians were not initially subject to its laws.

Over time, the plebeians acquired and learned to exercise greater authority, for the tribunes had the power to veto measures of the Senate. Eventually, plebeians were allowed to serve in the various offices of the cursus honorum, and by 287 B.C. the laws passed by the Consilium Plebis were made binding on all citizens.

As Rome expanded, the army played an increasingly significant role in Roman society. Beyond fulfilling the traditional military functions of protecting and annexing territory, the Roman legions built roads, bridges, and aqueducts. Under the general Gaius Marius, plebeians and noncitizens joined the army in large numbers, and many men made a career of military service. Those without land or citizenship received both upon retirement.

The emergence of a new class called the "equites," or equestrians, accompanied the army's growth. Military campaigns and the expansion of Roman territories opened up new opportunities for those patricians who found the world of business more appealing than the world of soldiering or politics. Though these equites were financially well-off, they sometimes aligned themselves politically with the plebeians against the senatorial order.

Despite occasional support from the equestrians, however, the plebeians faced many challenges. Small farmers found it increasingly difficult to compete with the patrician-owned plantations called "latifundia," which were cultivated chiefly by slaves captured in war. Indeed, the riches of conquest went disproportionately into the hands of the already wealthy, broadening the gap between rich and poor. Corruption was rampant, and plebeians and equestrians alike struggled to gain greater political clout. Predictably, they encountered resistance.

In a successful attempt to solidify the power of the Senate, the general Lucius Cornelius Sulla assumed the dictatorship from 82 to 79 B.C. Perfectly willing to murder anyone who opposed him, Sulla even drew up proscription lists of those he wanted killed—some 400 senators and 1,600 equites according to one estimate, 9,000 according to another.[1] Relations among the three orders could not have been worse.

After the death of Sulla in 78, there was further turmoil. The tribunes were agitating for the restoration of their full powers; pirates threatened the seas; Mithradates, king of Pontus, threatened the Roman provinces; and Spartacus led his famous slave revolt. In time, the tribunician power was restored, Pompey the Great subdued the pirates, Mithradates returned home, and Marcus Licinius Crassus conquered the slave revolt, but the fabric of Roman society was fraying.

In 64, an assassination plot threatened to topple the republic completely. Lucius Sergius Catilina, or "Catiline,"

Spartacus

In 73 B.C., Spartacus, a Thracian slave, escaped from the compound in Capua where his owners were training him to become a gladiator. Taking a few of his fellow "students" with him, Spartacus began one of the largest slave revolts in history. By 72, he had assembled more than 70,000 men, who successfully defeated every Roman legion they encountered. Crassus, one of the consuls in 72, took up arms against the rebellion, but he, too, was defeated twice. With six full legions, Crassus again set out against Spartacus and ultimately prevailed. As punishment, 6,000 of the rebellious slaves were crucified along the Appian Way, the main road in the Roman Empire.

Director Stanley Kubrick memorably captured the story of Spartacus in a 1960 film featuring Kirk Douglas as Spartacus, Laurence Olivier as Crassus, and an all-star cast including Jean Simmons, Charles Laughton, Peter Ustinov, and Tony Curtis. Based on a novel by Howard Fast, the film is not entirely accurate in all of its details, but nevertheless convincingly captures the character of the period and includes some magnificent cinematography, for which the film won an Academy Award.

a corrupt nobleman with a ruthless ambition, had unsuccessfully run for the consulship of 63. Dissatisfied with the election results, he assembled a band of conspirators and plotted to kill the duly elected consuls, along with many of their supporters in the Senate, and seize power for himself. Marcus Tullius Cicero, one of the consuls in 63, discovered the plan and successfully prosecuted the conspirators. The republic was safe, at least for the moment, and Cicero quickly took full credit, writing, "O lucky Rome, born on the date of my consulship!" Ironically, the republic that Cicero saved would eventually be toppled by a man born on September 23 of that very year: Gaius Octavius, the son of Atia, Julius Caesar's niece.

Other conflicts also contributed to the fleeting nature of this victory. In 52, when Pompey returned from a glorious campaign in the East, the Senate refused to ratify his actions and denied his soldiers the land grants that had long been one of the most important rewards for military service. At the same time, the Senate rejected a tax reassessment proposal of Crassus. Also rebuffed in 62 was Gaius Julius Caesar, who had just completed a campaign of his own in Spain. Caesar wanted a "triumph," a formal victory parade for a returning general. The Senate, however, would not let him run for the consulship of 61 unless he first resigned his generalship. The effective result was that Caesar had to forgo his triumph.

Still smarting from the Catilinarian conspiracy of 63, the senators may have feared that men such as Pompey, Caesar, and Crassus wanted too much power for themselves and therefore would be a threat to the authority of the Senate. On the other hand, the rebuffs of 62 seemed petty and may have actually emboldened the men to form an alliance against the Senate.

THE FIRST TRIUMVIRATE

In 60 B.C., Caesar, Pompey, and Crassus formed a secret political alliance, which we now know as the First Triumvirate. According to historian H.H. Scullard the alliance had no basis in Roman law and was called a conspiracy by some ancient writers.[2] Indeed, Cicero even feared, with some justification, that it would bring about the end of the republic.

In order for the triumvirate to succeed, it members would need to add some official public office to their already widening sphere of private influence. In 59, Caesar was elected consul. In this position, he was able to advance the agendas of Pompey and Crassus, as well as his own.

One of Caesar's first acts was to introduce a farm bill that would have provided land for Pompey's veterans. The bill was actually good public policy and consistent with the values and traditions of the republic, but the Senate was unimpressed. Fearing that passage of the bill would serve the political interests of Caesar and Pompey, they rejected the measure. Caesar, however, was not without recourse, and he took the bill before the popular assembly, which promptly approved it. Just for spite, he added a provision that would give even more land to the veterans. The resulting "*Lex Campana,*" as it was called, was a deliberate affront to the Senate but also a less sound economic measure than the original bill, for it confiscated the land from civilian owners and thus deprived the Roman Treasury of needed revenues, said Scullard.[3] In other measures, Pompey's eastern settlements and Crassus's tax bill were also ratified, effectively reversing the senatorial snubs of previous years. Finally, the alliance between Caesar and Pompey was strengthened by the marriage of Caesar's daughter Julia to his triumviral colleague.

Marc Antony, Caesar's co-consul, was typical of the statesmen produced by the Roman republican system. Such politicians worked their way up through the *cursus honorum*, gaining prestige and influence.

Upon completion of his term as consul, Caesar received the governorship of Cisalpine Gaul, and in 58, he began his famous Gallic campaign. That same year, Clodius, one of Cicero's enemies, became Tribune of the People, and he used that authority to get Cicero and another senator, Cato, out of Rome. The triumvirs, who supported Clodius, no doubt hoped that the Senate would be less of an obstacle for them when two of its leading members had been removed.

Soon, however, some tension emerged within the alliance. Clodius, at the secret urging of Crassus, began to agitate Pompey, who in turn decided to work for the return of Cicero. Meanwhile, Caesar was occupied in Gaul and needed Pompey and Crassus to hold things together in Rome until he could return. In April 56, the triumvirs met at Luca and achieved at least a partial reconciliation. Pompey and Crassus would serve as consuls, and they agreed to support an extension of Caesar's command in Gaul.

In 54, however, the alliance began to fray beyond repair. Julia died that year, and Pompey rejected a subsequent offer from Caesar for a second marriage alliance. In 53, there was open rioting in Rome, which Pompey was given the authority to subdue; no consuls were elected until July. In the province of Syria, the Parthians were a growing threat, and Crassus took command of Roman forces in the region but was killed at Carrhae. The three were now two; the triumvirate was now a duovirate.

Pompey served as sole consul until August 52, while Caesar was engaged in some of the most important battles of his Gallic campaign. With Caesar away from Rome for a few years, Pompey's authority and influence grew, and the Senate was even considering the recall of Caesar from his province, since the Parthian threat had not yet been eliminated. Although the bill demanding Caesar's recall failed to pass, the Senate did resolve that he and Pompey should each contribute one legion to Syria. Because Pompey had already given one of his legions to Caesar, he chose that one as his contribution to the Parthian campaign, effectively depriving Caesar of two legions.

This specific story is typical of the tensions mounting between Pompey and Caesar. By November 50, the consul Marcellus sided with Pompey and placed him in command of all forces in Italy. Shortly thereafter, Caesar decided that he had successfully brought the entire province of Gaul under Roman control and reorganized its local leaders. Contrary to Roman law, he led his army across the Rubicon River into Italy, effectively announcing open civil war with Pompey.

From the standpoint of numbers and political support in Rome, Pompey held a distinct advantage, for Caesar had only his Gallic legions. Pompey, by contrast, controlled Spain, the provinces of the East, and a strong naval force. Caesar's only advantage was that his army was now actually in Italy. Hardened by the Gallic Wars, the legions were able to advance toward Rome during the winter of 49. When Lucius Domitius Ahenobarbus, Caesar's successor in Gaul, added his armies to Caesar's, Pompey's position in Italy became untenable. The consuls and senators had already fled Rome, and Pompey had little choice but to retreat—first to Brundisium, then to Greece. Despite weaknesses elsewhere in the empire, Caesar's domination of Italy would prove crucial to his ultimate victory in the civil war.

With Italy secure, Caesar turned his attention to Spain, bringing several important towns under his control. By the end of 49, with the consular elections for 48 uncertain, Caesar was appointed dictator for 11 days. This appointment most likely carried more limited authority than Sulla's dictatorship,[4] according to Scullard, and perhaps was a mere expedient for conducting the elections. Whatever the case, Caesar quickly abandoned the dictatorship and was elected consul for 48.

The civil war now shifted east. Pompey was based in Greece, and Caesar set out from Rome to force an

The First Triumvirate of Caesar, Pompey, and Crassus broke up when Pompey tried to assume sole power. Caesar threatened civil war against Pompey by bringing his army across the Rubicon River, ominously close to the city of Rome.

engagement. Pompey, however, enjoyed several military advantages: He was better supplied, had more men, and had a highly mobile and effective navy. Accordingly, he decided to go on the offensive and attack Caesar near Dyrrhachium. Caesar's men withstood the attack but were forced to withdraw to Pharsalus. Pompey followed.

Confident in the strength of his numbers, Pompey attacked. An intensely brutal battle ensued, which the poet Lucan immortalized in his epic poem *De Bello Civili* (*On the Civil War*), also known as the *Pharsalia*. In Book 7, Caesar surveys the carnage:

> He sees rivers running fast with gore, and heaps of corpses like high hills; he beholds piles of the dead settling down into corruption, and counts the nations that followed Magnus [Pompey]. . . . In bloodshed, he sees his victorious fortune and the favour of Heaven.[5]

Caesar, a brilliant tactician and charismatic commander, won the day despite the long odds. Pompey fled to Egypt, where he was promptly executed by King Ptolemy, whom he had earlier supported but who now saw political advantage in befriending Julius Caesar.

Despite the defeat at Pharsalus, history has judged Pompey kindly. Scullard wrote that Cicero once remarked, "I cannot fail to mourn his fate, for I knew him to be an honorable, moral, and great man."[6] The support of Cicero and his close ties to the Senate have led many to suspect that Pompey was motivated as much by a desire to defend the republic as by his own thirst for power and glory. Scullard concluded, "His gifts as a soldier and administrator raised him above his contemporaries and made him a worthy opponent of Caesar; he lacked only that final spark of genius that set Caesar apart."[7]

Before returning to Italy, Caesar needed to establish a sense of order in Egypt, which was under the rule of the Macedonian teenagers Ptolemy XIII and his sister-wife, Cleopatra. Cleopatra, who was more intelligent and less beautiful than Hollywood would have us believe, was the senior ruler and soon became Caesar's mistress. Their brief affair was interrupted, however, by fighting in Asia Minor, when the son of Mithradates began to stir up trouble for the Romans. Julius Caesar subdued the uprising in a five-day war, whose decisive swiftness was well captured by the general in his famous phrase, "*Veni, Vidi, Vici* (I came, I saw, I conquered)."

When Caesar's consulship expired at the end of 48, he was appointed dictator for a second time. Because he spent much of the year in Asia Minor and later in combating Pompey's former allies in Africa, a new leader was needed to take charge in Rome. That responsibility fell to the young Marc Antony, the "Master of the Horse" and Caesar's chief deputy.

In 46, Caesar again served as consul while retaining his title of dictator. It was during this period that he advanced his domestic agenda, which included a reform of the Roman calendar that gave it the basic form we still recognize today.

The next year, Caesar won his fourth consulship and an official renewal of the dictatorship. It was now clear that Julius Caesar had become the sole and undisputed ruler of the entire Roman world. In 44, he was appointed *Dictator Perpetuus*, or "Dictator for Life."

It is important to remember that the dictatorship, though extraordinary, was nevertheless a constitutionally sanctioned office. Indeed, the Roman people, as well as Caesar himself, were adamant about avoiding a return to monarchy, and they maintained at least the external trappings of a republic. In a scene made famous by Shakespeare, Caesar refused to have himself crowned king:

> I saw Mark Antony offer him a crown—yet 't was not a crown neither, 't was one of these coronets—and, as I told you, he put it by once; but, for all that, to my thinking, he would fain have had it. Then he offered it to him again; then he put it by again; but, to my thinking, he was very loath to lay his fingers off it. And then he offered it the third time; he put it the third time by. . . .[8]

Modern and ancient historians alike cannot agree upon the meaning of Caesar's refusal. Some believe that he orchestrated the entire incident for his own political advantage. Perhaps he secretly wished to become a king, or perhaps he was genuinely opposed to the idea of kingship, as his own public comments would indicate.

What is undeniably clear, however, is that many in Rome opposed Caesar's autocracy in any form, whether as general, consul, dictator, or king. Indeed, pride and arrogance seemed to have gotten the better of Caesar in recent years, and many feared that he was becoming, or perhaps had already become, a tyrant. The very premise of republican government—that power should be shared and that the Senate and people of Rome should have the final say—was at stake.

THE ASSASSINATION

A group of conspirators, perhaps 60 or more in number, was formed for the specific purpose of removing Caesar from power, a goal that could only be accomplished by his death. The two leaders of the conspiracy were Gaius Cassius Longinus (known as "Cassius") and Marcus Junius Brutus (known as "Brutus"), who chose the Ides of March

(March 15) of 44 B.C. for the assassination. It is remarkable that Caesar, a political survivor and a man with many friends and allies, never heard of the plot, and even the ancient sources question the validity of the story of a soothsayer who allegedly told Caesar to "beware the Ides of March." More plausible is the story that Caesar's wife, Calpurnia, feared for her husband's life, but whatever warnings he may have received did not stop Caesar from proceeding to the Senate as scheduled.

The conspirators, whose togas concealed their daggers, surrounded the dictator and stabbed him to death. Because Caesar had once pardoned Brutus for supporting Pompey at Pharsalus, he may well have considered this conspirator's blow "the most unkindest cut of all," as Shakespeare famously put it. Indeed, there is good ancient support for the legend that Caesar spoke to Brutus, saying, "You too, my son?" (Shakespeare's "*et tu, Brute?*"), but he probably would have spoken in Greek, and the actual words he used may have meant something more like, "same to you, boy!"

Shortly thereafter, Gaius Julius Caesar died. Though he fell short of becoming a true emperor, Caesar nevertheless set the pattern of military and political leadership that would be followed by subsequent rulers.

Caesar was assassinated in 44 B.C. and Marc Antony became the legal head of state. He gave a moving speech at Caesar's funeral that convinced the public masses to drive the assassins out of the city. Antony then gained even more power.

The Second Triumvirate

Although Caesar's murderers had succeeded in eliminating a dictator, the question of who would govern Rome for the future remained very much unresolved. As Caesar's co-consul, Marcus Antonius (Marc Antony) was the legal head of state, and Marcus Aemilius Lepidus, the *Magister Equitum*, or "Master of the Horse," also wielded considerable power. Nevertheless, it was not a sure bet that either of these men could govern Rome even in the short term, to say nothing of their ability to secure for themselves a more lasting power.

Even before the assassination, two leading political factions were beginning to emerge: the "Caesarians," who supported Julius Caesar, and the "republicans," who opposed him. Some of the loyalty and opposition to Caesar was personal, but there was also a philosophical divide. The Caesarians tended to believe that the increasing scope and complexity of the Roman world demanded a single, strong leader. Furthermore, many Caesarians also felt that a dictator could actually serve the interests of the average citizen by rooting out corruption among the senators and lesser magistrates. The republicans, by contrast, were reluctant to place too much power into the hands of one man and therefore sympathized with the conspirators' efforts to restore Rome to its traditional republican form of government, in which power was shared and the Senate was the chief governing body.

Faced with a turbulent and divided Rome, Antony knew he had to act decisively. He immediately gained possession of Caesar's papers and estate and persuaded Lepidus to bring some of his troops into the city for the purpose of establishing and maintaining order. A compromise of sorts was then reached in the Senate: The conspirators would receive amnesty but Caesar would have a state funeral. In addition, all of his decrees would be allowed to stand, and the provisions of his will would be followed. In his will, Caesar named his grandnephew, Gaius Octavius, as his heir. Octavius received three-fourths of Caesar's estate, but Caesar's gardens and a substantial sum of money, 300 sesterces apiece, were left to the people of Rome.

At Caesar's funeral, Antony gave an eloquent speech recorded by the ancient historian Plutarch and immortalized by Shakespeare. In the speech, Antony managed to turn public sentiment against the conspirators, and an angry mob drove Brutus and Cassius from Rome.

With two of the chief murderers gone, Antony was able to amass considerable power. He gave his ally Lepidus the prestigious office of *Pontifex Maximus*, or "Chief Priest," and formed an important alliance with Sextus Pompeius (the son of Pompey the Great), who was in command of six legions in Spain. In addition, Antony secured the province of Syria for his new co-consul, Dolabella, and Macedonia for himself. At Antony's urging, the Senate abolished the office of dictator, provided lands for Caesar's veterans, and approved all of Caesar's acts, including some measures of Antony's own creation, which he falsely attributed to the late dictator.

It soon become clear that, although the conspirators had succeeded in killing Julius Caesar and were able to avoid execution themselves, they had failed in their ultimate goal of restoring true republican government. The dictator was gone, but in his place Antony had amassed an alarmingly great amount of personal power.

When Octavius learned of his great-uncle's murder, he hastened to Rome from Apollonia, where he was engaged in military service. En route, the 19-year-old learned that he was Caesar's heir and promptly adopted the name Gaius Julius Caesar Octavianus (shortened to "Octavian" by modern historians). He thought, plausibly enough, that Antony would want to help him avenge Caesar's murder, but Antony saw the young Octavian as a potential rival for power and was unwilling to cooperate.

All along, Antony had been playing both ends against the middle where the conspirators were concerned: First, he secured an amnesty for them, but then, he incited the citizens to drive them from Rome. Now, he would take a similar approach with Octavian: Caesar's will would be formally ratified, but he would not follow all of its provisions. In particular, Antony refused to release Caesar's assets to Octavian, the dictator's legal heir. Meanwhile, Antony continued to build his own military power base by gaining control of Transalpine and Cisalpine Gaul as a substitute for Macedonia. Since he retained control of the Macedonian legions, or soldiers, however, the loss of administrative control of the province didn't mean much.

These actions began to alarm Cicero, a senator and one of Rome's leading republicans. Because Cicero had been instrumental in foiling the Catilinarian conspiracy of 63, one might have expected the senator to condemn the conspiracy of 44; however, the plot to kill Caesar was of a different nature, in Cicero's eyes. In this case, the murdered man was an enemy of the Republic. Thus, Cicero was among those who advised Antony to spare the conspirators. He hoped that Antony would serve not only as a peace-maker but also as a champion of republican values. The senator was quickly disappointed. In May 44, Cicero wrote to his friend Atticus about "the crushed or rather non-existent republic" and called Antony "so unprincipled, so disgraceful, and so mischievous, that at times one almost wishes for Caesar back again."[9]

Cicero

Marcus Tullius Cicero, born in Arpinum on January 3, 106 B.C., was perhaps the world's first celebrity lawyer. During his 40-year career, he prosecuted several high-profile cases, including the impeachment of the Sicilian Governor Gaius Verres on charges of extortion. Most of the time, however, Cicero represented the defendant. His clients included many politicians charged with various forms of corruption; Marcus Caelius, who was accused (and probably guilty) of theft and murder; and the poet Archias, who had been one of Cicero's teachers. We know of more than 100 trials in which Cicero was involved, but there may have been many more.

Cicero's work as a trial lawyer would have earned him enduring fame even if he had accomplished nothing else in life, but the celebrated advocate was a man of many talents. He held every office of the cursus honorum, served a term as governor of the province Cilicia, and was a leading member of the Senate. In addition, Cicero was a prolific writer, composing works of political and moral philosophy, theology, and the art of rhetoric. As a poet, Cicero translated Greek works into Latin and composed several poems about the important events of his times, including his own consulship.

Cicero was the ideal educated Roman. His varied careers included writer, poet, lawyer, and statesman. His politics were complicated; he helped reveal the Catilinarian conspiracy yet urged leniency for the conspirators involved in Caesar's murder.

By 43, Cicero had had enough. He delivered a series of speeches against Antony and persuaded the Senate to send Octavian and the consuls Hirtius and Pansa against him. The campaign was successful, and Antony was defeated in battles at Forum Gallorum, located between Mutina and Bononia (modern Modena and Bologna) in northern Italy. Hirtius and Pansa died in these battles, leaving Octavian in command of their armies.

Instead of rewarding Octavian for his victory, the Senate took Antony's defeat as a vindication of the conspirators' actions and rewarded them. Brutus received a command in Macedonia, Cassius in Syria, and Decimus Brutus took charge of the consular armies previously under Octavian's control. Sextus Pompeius, a powerful general who was not among the conspirators, was put in command of a fleet. These terms did not please Octavian, who refused to relinquish control of the consular armies. He marched on Rome, where, backed by the might of eight legions, he saw to it that he was elected consul.

With power divided so many ways, Antony's military might was still quite formidable. Lepidus remained an important ally, and Antony also enlisted the aid of two generals, Caius Asinius Pollio and Lucas Munatius Plancus, whose troops gave him effective control over Spain and Gaul. Decimus Brutus, caught in the power struggle between Octavian and Antony, lost the support of his own troops and attempted to flee to Greece but was killed along the way. Brutus and Cassius, however, still controlled substantial forces in the East, with which they might continue to pursue the republican cause.

Four factions were now competing for control: Antony and his allies in the West, Octavian in Italy, Brutus and Cassius in the East, and Sextus Pompeius at sea. Octavian realized that the only way to eliminate the murderers of Julius Caesar was to form an alliance with Antony. Quintus Pedius, Octavian's co-consul, passed a bill that lifted the condemnation of Antony and Lepidus, revoked the amnesty of Brutus and Cassius, and affirmed Octavian as Caesar's legitimate heir.

On an island in the middle of a river near Bologna, Octavian met with Antony and Lepidus in November 43. There they formed what came to be known as the Second Triumvirate, an alliance that far surpassed the first in terms of raw political and military power. While Julius Caesar's alliance with Pompey and Crassus was little more than a gentlemen's agreement of mutual cooperation, Octavian's triumvirate was a formal power-sharing arrangement to be sanctioned by the rule of law. On November 27, 43 B.C., the Senate passed a bill in which Octavian, Antony, and Lepidus were declared *"Triumviri Rei Publicae Constituendae"* and empowered to legislate and make official appointments for a period of five years without seeking Senate approval for each decision. Each triumvir was also given a provincial command: Antony received Transalpine and Cisalpine Gaul; Lepidus received the rest of Gaul and Spain; and Octavian received Africa, Sicily, and Sardinia. Lepidus became consul in 42, while Antony and Octavian set out against Brutus and Cassius in the East.

In the mounting conflict between Brutus and Octavian leading up to the Battle of Philippi, even coins were used as propaganda to emphasize their opposite positions. This ancient coin shows images of Caesar and Octavian.

Philippi

O n January 1, 42 B.C., the Senate recognized the now-dead
Julius Caesar as a god, resolved to uphold all of his acts as
dictator, and commissioned a new temple of Divus Julius
to be built at the site of his funeral pyre in the Roman Forum. These
measures were particularly advantageous to Octavian, who was
now free to adopt the title of *Divi Filius* ("son of a god") and who
received further justification, if any was needed, for pursuing the
murderers of his adoptive father.

While Octavian was eager to assume the role of Divi Filius,
Brutus was no less eager to be viewed as the man who freed Rome
from the clutches of a dictator. Indeed, the status of Julius Caesar's
memory in the eyes of the public was crucial for determining

whether or not Rome would remain a true republic. If Caesar was a god, all of his actions would be justified, and people might more readily accept another powerful, charismatic leader, especially his heir. His assassins, moreover, would have to be killed. If, however, he was remembered as an overreaching dictator, the conspirators would be cast as defenders of a republic still worth fighting for and their actions against Caesar would be vindicated, while the triumvirs would be viewed as potential dictators. The stakes could not have been higher. Both sides tried to sway public opinion and even issued coins with images emphasizing their respective positions, but it would ultimately take an armed conflict to resolve the issue.

By the year 42, Brutus and Cassius had managed to assemble substantial armies in the East. Through a combination of military victories, plunder, taxation, and extortion, the two conspirators amassed 19 legions, a formidable navy, and enough supplies for a long campaign. They met near the Macedonian town of Philippi on the Via Egnatia and set up camp in September 42.

The terrain at Philippi presented difficulties that Brutus and Cassius turned to their defensive advantage. Each pitched a camp on a separate hill. Brutus's camp had a mountainous terrain behind it that would impede an enemy's approach, and Cassius's camp was flanked by marshland that would be equally treacherous to cross. The republicans would need these good defenses if their 19 legions, many of them undermanned, were to have any chance of success against the 28 legions of Octavian and Antony. Despite being outnumbered, however, Brutus and Cassius enjoyed two more advantages: They had the superior cavalry—20,000 to Antony's 13,000—and they were well stocked with supplies, which meant that a protracted stand-off could work in their favor.

For several days in late September and early October,

Antony lined up his troops as if to threaten battle. Brutus and Cassius, with time on their side, did not come out to meet him. Antony must have anticipated such a reaction, for while the main part of his army stood ready for battle, a small detachment circled around to the far side of the marsh and began to build a causeway over the swampy terrain to provide a means of approach for an unexpected attack from the side.

On October 3, Antony began his attack by sending troops across the now accessible marsh. Cassius, who wrongly supposed that the marsh itself would thwart such an attack, had positioned few soldiers on the marsh side of his camp, which Antony captured with relative ease. Nevertheless, the loss of the camp did not prevent Cassius from engaging Antony's forces on the plain. The republicans fought valiantly but were eventually beaten back by the triumvir. Then Cassius received word that Brutus had also been defeated and, fearing that escape was impossible, ordered his shield-bearer to kill him.

In point of fact, however, Brutus and his forces were faring quite well in a separate contest with Octavian, whose camp they eventually captured. As it happened, Octavian was ill on the day of battle and might have been killed but for a strange coincidence. According to the ancient soldier-turned-historian Velleius Paterculus,

> Caesar [Octavianus] was performing his duties as commander although he was in the poorest of health, and had been urged not to remain in camp by Artorius his physician, who had been frightened by a warning which had appeared to him in his sleep.[10]

Other ancient sources suggest that Octavian was actually hiding in a marsh during the attack. Whatever the case, he survived the battle but failed to topple Brutus.

On October 23, a second Battle of Philippi was fought.

Despite the loss of Cassius, time was on Brutus's side. He still had plenty of supplies and also controlled the seas. It was therefore possible for him to block supplies and reinforcements from ever reaching his opponents.

His men, however, were confident and eager for a fight, so Brutus let them engage the enemy. The right wing, commanded by Brutus himself and bolstered by a strong cavalry, fought successfully. The rest of the line, however, had been stretched out to match the length of Antony's forces. This maneuver prevented the republican army from being outflanked but weakened the line, thus allowing Antony to penetrate the center and attack Brutus's right wing from the rear. Seeing his troops defeated, Brutus took flight and killed himself.

Octavian quickly rounded up all those who were involved in the assassination of Julius Caesar and had them summarily executed. The brutality and sometimes merciless savagery of the executions alarmed even ancient observers. Then-contemporary biographer Suetonius told the story of a father and son who pleaded for their lives:

> When two others, father and son, begged for their lives, he [Octavian] is said to have bidden them cast lots or play mora [a game in which contestants thrust out their fingers, and the one who correctly names the number thrust out by the other is the winner] to decide which should be spared. He then looked on while both died, since the father was executed because he offered to die for his son, and the [son] thereupon took his own life. Because of this, the rest [of the defeated soldiers] . . . saluted Antony respectfully as Imperator ["victorious general"] when they were led out in chains, but abused Octavian to his face with the foulest abuse.[11]

In fairness, the victory at Philippi really was Antony's, but

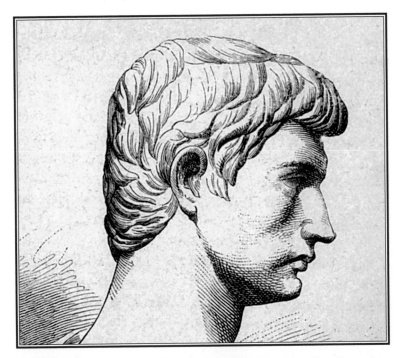

Brutus conspired to kill Caesar yet managed to stay alive through political intrigue and power struggles in the Senate. He aligned himself with Cassius and the two took on Antony at Philippi. Brutus killed himself in 42 B.C. when defeat was certain at the second Battle of Philippi.

that did not stop Octavian from taking credit. "Twice I defeated in battle those who slew my father," he wrote in his *Res Gestae*, or *Book of Accomplishments*.[12]

The defeat of Brutus and Cassius at Philippi had dramatic consequences, not just for Octavian but for the future of Rome. As the historian Appian put it, "the form of [the Romans'] government was decided chiefly by that day's work, and they have not gone back to democracy yet."[13] It was by no means clear in 42 that Octavian would emerge as the sole leader of Rome, but the Republic was dead and the triumvirs' hold on power secure. It was only a matter of time before Antony and Octavian would find themselves on opposite sides of a colossal power struggle.

Sextus
Pompeius

4

The solid foundations of ancient Rome's magnificent buildings belied the swiftly shifting power base after Caesar's death.

After Philippi, the triumvirs were challenged, in the words of Scullard, by one more "competitor for power:"[14] Sextus Pompeius, who occupied a unique position in the years between the death of Caesar and the Battle of Actium. As the son of Pompey the Great, he had fought with his father in the civil wars against Julius Caesar. Indeed, he was one of the few Pompeians to have even survived. It was therefore logical to suppose that he would have been a natural ally of the conspirators, and after Philippi, many of the supporters of Brutus and Cassius did join forces with Sextus.

The fact that Sextus Pompeius and the conspirators had shared a common enemy in the past, however, did not mean that they shared a common vision of the future. The assassins of Julius Caesar had acted to end a dictatorship and restore the Republic. Sextus Pompeius seems to have had no such intent, although his precise motivations are still disputed by modern historians. The leading view is that Sextus was something of an "adventurer," more interested in the glory of military victory than in ruling Rome or even influencing the selection of a future leader. Indeed, if he had any thoughts of playing the role of kingmaker in the battles between Antony and Octavian, he cannot have been happy with his choices. Antony was involved with Cleopatra, Caesar's former mistress and a woman instrumental in the death of Sextus's father. Octavian, as Caesar's heir, was no better, and Lepidus had served at Caesar's right hand as "Master of the Horse."

If Sextus wasn't interested in choosing among Antony, Octavian, and Lepidus, and if he had no desire to rule Rome himself, he may have hoped for a four-way alliance with these other leaders. While the prospective triumvirs were working out their power-sharing arrangements, Sextus Pompeius was building a military power base of his own. In 42, he had defeated Salvidienus, a commander loyal to Octavian, at the Straits of Messina, and by 40, Sicily and Sardinia were under his control. His fleet had also successfully combated the pirates operating throughout the Mediterranean. As master of the seas, Sextus became something of a pirate himself, interfering with Rome's grain supply, no doubt as a way of blackmailing the triumvirs into giving him more power.

His plan seemed to be working, at least temporarily. The shortage of grain in Rome produced mob riots, and Octavian himself was actually attacked with stones.[15] When Sextus met the triumvirs at Misenum in 39, he secured official control of Corsica, along with Sicily and Sardinia, for a period of five years. In addition, he was promised

Peloponesus plus a consulship in 35, when his command would expire. Finally, the troops who sided with Sextus Pompeius after Philippi would be granted full amnesty. In return, Sextus would protect the grain supply and keep out of Italy.

This "alliance" was both uneasy and short-lived. Pompey did not receive control of the Peloponesus and therefore did not restore the grain supply. Then, in 38, Menas, the governor of Sardinia, turned that province over to Octavian, who, on January 17, had just divorced his wife, Scribonia, the aunt of Sextus Pompeius's wife (also called Scribonia), to marry Livia Drusilla. This marriage seems to have been motivated by genuine love, with the added benefit of Livia's powerful family and political connections, but the divorce of Scribonia deepened the animosity between Sextus Pompeius and Octavian, who soon found themselves in a state of open warfare.

The first battle came at Cumae that same year. Having lost Menas, Sextus put Menecrates, a long-standing enemy of the defector, in charge of the fleet. Octavian's forces were led by Calvisius and Cornificus, with Menas serving under Calvisius. Menecrates had hoped for an engagement farther out to sea, but when Calvisius and Cornificus could not be driven from the shore, Menecrates attacked, pinning his opponents against the rocks and destroying many ships in what amounted to a land battle. During the fighting, Menas mortally wounded Menecrates and was wounded himself in the process. Menas, the defector, survived the encounter but later lost his ship and jumped into the sea and drowned rather than face capture. When the fleet of Pompeius set sail from Cumae, Calvisius decided to give chase but lost nearly half of his ships in a storm. Gratified by his success and good fortune, Sextus Pompeius declared himself the "son of Neptune," god of the sea.

Octavian realized that he would need to strengthen his

Agrippa was given the task of building a Roman navy for Octavian to meet the ships of Sextus Pompeius, another challenger to the Second Triumvirate's control of the empire. A new harbor, new ships, and new weapons were all constructed under Agrippa's direction.

navy if he hoped for better odds against Sextus. For this task he enlisted the aid of Marcus Agrippa, an accomplished admiral and a friend, who had just returned from Gaul to assume the consulship for the year 37 B.C. To accommodate a new fleet, Agrippa build a huge harbor near Naples by dredging Lake Lucrinus, excavating to increase the depth, and then joining it to Lake Avernus, thereby extending this new lake to the sea in order to form the great harbor that he named the Portus Julius. Ship construction began, and Agrippa even arranged to free 20,000 slaves, whom he then recruited to serve as rowers in the new navy. The admiral also made advances in weaponry. He improved a grappling hook called the harpax and increased the range of his catapults. The entire process of creating the harbor, building the ships, and training the men took only a year and a half, a remarkably short time for an undertaking of such complexity. In July 36, Octavian would be ready to engage Sextus Pompeius in Sicily.

Octavian's plan was to attack Sicily from several directions at once. He and Agrippa would sail down from Portus Julius and attack Sextus's fleet off the northeastern coast of the island. Lepidus, who was stationed in Africa, would mount a land attack in western Sicily, supported by 120 of Antony's ships under the command of Statilius Taurus. As it happened, a storm prevented Statilius from ever reaching the island, but Lepidus was nevertheless successful in his mission. Storms also delayed the arrival of Agrippa and Octavian, who established a base at Strongyle (modern-day Stromboli).

When scouts discovered a large portion of Sextus Pompeius's fleet near Mylae, Octavian devised a new plan. He assumed that Sextus was present at Mylae and that Tauromenium was therefore vulnerable. Leaving Agrippa to deal with the fleet, Octavian sailed with three legions to meet Statilius Taurus and prepared to invade Tauromenium. He arrived with his infantry under the command of Cornificus and demanded that the town surrender. Sextus Pompeius must have figured out Octavian's strategy, for he arrived with a large fleet just as Octavian's men were beginning to set up camp. On land, Cornificus managed to hold his camp but suffered losses at the hands of Pompeius's cavalry. At sea, victory was more decisive for Sextus, who destroyed or captured most of Octavian's ships. Octavian himself only narrowly escaped.

Meanwhile, Agrippa was having greater success at Mylae. He sailed first to the island of Hiera and defeated the Pompeian soldiers stationed there. Before dawn the next day, he took half of his fleet to attack the 40 ships of Demochares, Sextus's lieutenant. When Sextus realized that Agrippa was planning to attack, he hastened to Mylae with 70 ships of his own and sent for reinforcements from Messana—45 ships under the command of

Apollophanes. Agrippa called his remaining ships down from Mylae.

Each side enjoyed several advantages over the other. Sextus's men were better sailors and more experienced, and his short, light ships were quicker and more maneuverable. Agrippa's men were better soldiers, and his large, heavy ships were better at ramming and harder to damage. Appian described the battle tactics of the two commanders:

> [The Pompeian fleet] excelled not so much in close fighting as in the nimbleness of their movements, and they broke oar blades and rudders, cut off oar handles, or separated the enemy's ships entirely, doing them no less harm than by ramming. [Agrippa's men] sought to cut down with their beaks the hostile ships, which were smaller in size, or shatter them, or break through them. When they came to close quarters, being higher, they could hurl missiles down upon the enemy, and more easily throw the "ravens" and the grappling irons.[16]

Agrippa prevailed in most contests, sinking 30 Pompeian ships while losing only five of his own. Octavian's admiral hoped to finish off the enemy fleet, but Sextus Pompeius's men retreated to the shallower shoals, where Agrippa's larger ships could not safely follow. Eventually, they reluctantly withdrew.

Although Agrippa had won the day for Octavian, Sextus Pompeius still had a formidable fleet at his disposal and was not yet prepared to give up. He held the territory from Mylae to Naulochus and also maintained strongholds throughout Sicily. A decisive battle, he hoped, might drive Octavian from the island.

Meanwhile, Agrippa captured Tyndaris and chose that site as his new base of operations. Octavian soon joined him with 21 legions, 20,000 cavalry, and at least 5,000 light-armed troops. After an aborted attempt to attack the army of Tisenus, one of Sextus Pompeius's lieutenants, Octavian was forced to set up a makeshift camp near Mount Myconium. Without the protection of tents, the men spent the night in a fierce rainstorm as the fires of an erupting Mount Etna could be seen in the distance. For shelter, Octavian ordered shields to be held over him as he slept.

Working with Agrippa, Octavian achieved some success in a few minor skirmishes and hoped to provoke a decisive battle by cutting off Sextus's supplies. Instead of trying to blockade or intercept supply ships, however, Octavian decided to capture the towns that were providing the supplies in the first place. As expected, the move forced Sextus's hand.

Sextus Pompeius knew that his best chance of victory would come in a naval battle, so he formally challenged Octavian to just such a contest. At first, Octavian was reluctant to accept the proposal since, in the words of Appian, "he dreaded all naval encounters, which until now had turned out badly for him," but ultimately agreed since he "considered it base [or ignoble] to refuse."[17] They fixed the number of ships at 300 to a side and set a date.

The Battle of Naulochus, as it would come to be known, was fought on the open sea within sight of the Sicilian coast and with the opposing ships arranged in a long line. The actual combat was in many respects quite typical of naval warfare in the first century B.C. It began with the launching of missiles (stones, arrows, javelins, firebrands) and soon included ramming attacks. For a long time, neither side was able to gain a clear advantage, but the difference in the contest seems to have been the use of Agrippa's new grappling hook, which Sextus Pompeius's men had never encountered before and were unable to defend against. Because Octavian had the better soldiers, when the ships were drawn together, his side usually got the better of things.

Sextus Pompeius took on Octavian in the Battle of Naulochus and then, once defeated, fled to Asia, Marc Antony's territory. Marcus Titius captured and killed Sextus Pompeius there, thus ending this part of the struggle for control of Rome.

The clash of arms was both chaotic and terrifying. The battle was essentially part of a civil war, with Roman fighting against Roman. Nearly all of the soldiers spoke Latin, used the same weapons, and wore the same armor. Although the ships of Octavian and Sextus sailed under different colors, the men were virtually indistinguishable in appearance. To prevent "friendly fire" casualties, code words were exchanged, but it didn't take long for each side to learn the watchwords of the other and use them to trick their opponents. In all the confusion, it was hard to know whom to trust, and many a soldier perished at the hands of a mistaken ally.

By the end of the day, it was clear that Octavian and Agrippa had gained the upper hand. Only three of their ships were sunk, while the Pompeians lost 28. Agrippa made one last push, forcing Sextus to take flight. Only 17 of Sextus's ships escaped, many were either driven aground or burned and the rest surrendered.

After his defeat at Naulochus, Sextus Pompeius fled first to Messana, where part of his army was stationed, but because of defections he was forced to sneak in disguised as a private citizen. Once he had gathered his possessions, he sailed east, hoping to find a friend in Antony. Lepidus and Agrippa moved in to capture Messana while Octavian stayed on at Naulochus and chose not to pursue Pompeius. Appian speculated as to the reasons:

> Octavian neither pursued Pompeius nor allowed others
> to do so; either because he refrained from encroaching
> on Antony's dominions, or because he preferred to wait
> and see what Antony would do to Pompeius and make
> that a pretext for a quarrel if he should do wrong . . . or,
> as Octavian said later, because Pompeius was not one
> of his father's murderers.[18]

In Asia, Pompeius was able to raise three legions, which he used to defend himself against the attacks of Antony's generals. Although some of his friends and allies began to defect to Antony, Pompeius would not give in. Eventually, he was captured and executed by General Marcus Titius, thus eliminating the triumvirs' last major rival.[19]

The love affair and political partnership between Marc Antony and Cleopatra lasted for years. Octavian used this connection to cast public sentiment against Antony for his own gain.

5

Octavian versus Antony and Cleopatra

B y 33 B.C., Antony had established a firm and effective administrative control of the East. By backing those local leaders who would willingly cooperate with Rome, Antony set up a series of "client kingdoms" and reshaped provincial boundaries to suit the territories controlled by his favored monarchs. Military successes by Ventidius, Sosius, and Canidius, generals loyal to Antony, further helped his cause.

Parthia remained something of a sticking point, however. In 53, Crassus had suffered a crushing defeat at the hands of the Parthians, who even captured the Roman flags, or standards, in battle. The loss of the standards was regarded as a particular disgrace for Rome, and their recovery would have represented an important military and political victory for Antony. For years, he had been contemplating an invasion, and he thought he saw an opening in 36, when Phraates came to power by killing his relatives—a move that divided the Parthian court. When it came time to fight, however, the campaign turned out to be anything but a great success: Antony lost at least 20,000 infantry and 4,000 cavalry (perhaps a full quarter of his troops) and failed to recover the standards.

Having failed in Parthia, Antony turned his attention to the neighboring province, Armenia, in the hope that a victory there might help hold the Parthians in check. The "Armenian Campaign," however, turned out to be not much of a struggle. Antony captured Artavasdes, the Armenian king, and then sent in an army of occupation, which quickly subdued the province.

Although most historians regard this victory as a relatively modest accomplishment (perhaps, in part, because Octavian mocked it at the time), Antony nevertheless held a great celebration in his own honor—the notorious "Eastern triumph" of 34. Dressed as Dionysus (the Greek god of wine), Antony marched through the streets of Alexandria in a victory parade in which he dedicated spoils of war to the Egyptian gods. The parade was a version (and some might say a mocking version) of the traditional Roman triumph, in which a victorious general would dedicate the spoils of war to Jupiter Optimus Maximus (the leading Roman god). Some time after the parade, Antony gave certain choice Eastern lands to Cleopatra and her children in what came to be known as the "Donations of Alexandria."

We have no way of knowing precisely what the average man on the streets of Rome would have thought of these measures, but there seems to have been little negative reaction. Nevertheless, Octavian would skillfully manage to use Antony's actions against him in a highly effective propaganda campaign. Instead of going directly after

Antony, however, he attacked Cleopatra, alleging that she was bent on the domination of the Roman world. In Octavian's view, she had corrupted Antony and turned him into a decadent Eastern-style monarch whose loyalties now lay in Egypt rather than Rome. It must be mentioned that we really do not know how successful this propaganda was at the time. Indeed, it is possible that this negative view of Antony and Cleopatra only took root after Octavian defeated them at Actium, but there is no doubt that the young Caesar hoped to sway public opinion.

Although Octavian tried to capitalize on Antony's blunders, his own successes were almost certainly of greater consequence. By 33 B.C., he had successfully completed the wars in Illyricum, and many generals who supported him were equally successful in Spain and Africa. With these victories came financial resources, which Octavian wisely funneled into public works projects in Rome, including both new construction and the restoration of old temples, bath houses, and other public facilities. Under the supervision of Agrippa, there were substantial improvements to the aqueduct and sewer systems. These and other "quality of

S.P.Q.R.

The Roman people took great pride in their republican form of democracy. They steadfastly believed that the power to govern rested with the people themselves and with the Senate, which served as their chief legislative body. This belief was commonly expressed in the phrase, "The Senate and the People of Rome." Abbreviated *S.P.Q.R.*, the words in Latin are "Senatus Populusque Romanus."

The letters S.P.Q.R. appeared on some Roman coins and can still be seen today on ancient monuments throughout the Roman world. In addition, the current citizens of Rome honor their ancient heritage by placing "S.P.Q.R." on their city's manhole covers.

life" measures showed that Octavian could be a diligent and effective administrator. Not surprisingly, his actions won favor with the people and built up a reservoir of good will that Octavian would need if he ever hoped to emerge as the sole ruler of Rome.

The events of 32 B.C. would be crucial in shaping the context in which the final showdown between Antony and Octavian would be waged. Indeed, before 32 it was not a sure bet that there would even be a battle. While it is true that there had been a certain amount of animosity and mistrust between the two leading triumvirs, there were no signs that an outright military conflict was imminent.

Most scholars believe that the second term of the triumvirate, which had essentially become a duovirate, expired on December 31, 33 B.C., although that date cannot be unequivocally confirmed on the basis of existing ancient sources. Perhaps the official ending date was not even clear at the time. In any case, the supposed expiration seems to have had little effect on Antony, who continued to call himself triumvir and, as a semidivine king in Alexandria, presided over a vast Eastern empire. Octavian's hold on power in Italy was considerably more tenuous. Although he retained his provincial commands in Spain, Gaul, Africa, Sicily, and Sardinia, without the title of triumvir he would have no legal power in Rome or anywhere in Italy. Military power and personal influence certainly counted for something, but they would not be sufficient, especially since the two consuls for 32 were supporters of Antony: Gaius Sosius and Cnaeus Domitius Ahenobarbus. Furthermore, much of the Senate was still loyal to Antony and believed, rightly or wrongly, that he was the leader more likely to defend republican principles.

From the time he took office, Sosius openly opposed Octavian, and in February, he introduced a motion of censure against Caesar's heir. That motion, whose exact provisions remain uncertain, was vetoed by the tribune Nonius Balbus. The measure might not have passed anyway, but it clearly put Octavian on the defensive. He left Rome for a few weeks but returned with a military escort and claimed for himself a Senate seat between the two consuls. Sosius and Ahenobarbus immediately fled to Antony, accompanied by a large contingent of senators—at least 100 and perhaps as many as 300 of the approximately 1,000 men who comprised the Senate.

Both sides vied for supremacy in the public relations war. Antony organized a "Senate in Exile" to highlight what he viewed as Octavian's illegal usurpation of the Senate in Rome. Octavian branded Antony as an effeminate king given to extravagant luxury (for such was the stereotype of Eastern rulers). Indeed, Antony gave him ample ammunition for the charge, and the ancient historian Plutarch records Antony's penchant for decadent partying. In many ways, the conflict was shaping up as a clash between East and West, with Octavian claiming that Alexandrian decadence was a threat to Roman virtues and Antony and Cleopatra poised to defend the East against an overbearing, imperialist Rome.

As events played out during the year 32, Octavian emerged as having the better argument, at least in the eyes of the Roman public. Antony had been living with Cleopatra as his wife (and some say they were actually married in an Egyptian ceremony) in spite of the fact that he was still legally married to Octavia, the sister of Octavian. Ahenobarbus counseled Antony to send Cleopatra home and thus remove one arrow from Octavian's propaganda quiver; however, Antony reasoned, on the advice of Canidius Crassus, one of his leading generals, that armed conflict was increasingly likely and that Cleopatra's presence would be good for morale and would motivate the men to take up arms against Octavian's Roman forces. Thus,

The decadence of Alexandria is shown here in a painting by Maarten van Heemskerck. In 32 B.C., Octavian emphasized the city's (and therefore Cleopatra's) immorality and corruption. By association, Antony was also thought corrupt and unworthy to be a Roman ruler.

Cleopatra remained, and Antony sent Octavia a notice of divorce sometime in May or June of 32.

The divorce, which Octavian had been urging for some time, played right into his hands. Now Octavian had even more ammunition for his attack on Antony's character, portraying him as an adulterer who preferred a wanton Eastern queen to a virtuous Roman matron. The propaganda machine was in full force, and Antony's support in the Senate began to erode.

The final blow came when Titius and Plancus, two senators and one-time Antony supporters, saw the wind blowing in Octavian's direction and changed sides. They revealed that they had witnessed Antony's will, which was housed with the Vestal Virgins, and that exposing its contents would be advantageous to Octavian. To unseal the will of a living man would be a clear violation of Roman law, but Octavian opened it anyway and publicized its provisions, which stipulated that Antony was to be buried in Alexandria and included substantial gifts to his Egyptian children. Octavian is sometimes accused of having altered the will to suit his own needs, and it would not be out of character for him to do so, but since none of the will's provisions (as we have received them) appears to be in conflict with what we know about Antony, the charge is most likely false.

Octavian was now prepared for action, again choosing Cleopatra as his chief target on the theory that opposing her would win stronger public support than opposing Antony directly. At his urging, the Senate formally called Cleopatra an enemy of Rome and declared war against her. To drive the point home for the Roman people, Octavian performed an ancient ritual at the Temple of Bellona in which the citizens put on their military cloaks and symbolically prepared for war. The final battle would not occur for another year, but military conflict now seemed inevitable.

Roman Naval
Warfare

This painting shows the decline of the Carthaginian Empire. The 100 years of war with the Carthaginians forced the Romans to build their first navy. The remnants of this original naval force fell into the hands of Sextus Pompeius, leaving Octavian with nothing until Agrippa built a navy in 37–36 B.C.

HISTORY OF THE ROMAN NAVY

In the early days of the Republic, the Roman navy didn't amount to much. Rome's economy was largely agricultural, and imported goods could be brought to Italy by traders rather than the Romans themselves. If Rome ever needed to expand, that objective could be accomplished by land forces working in Italy to subdue the neighboring tribes. The chief threat of external attack came from the Gauls in the north, but they could also be repulsed by land forces. Rome, therefore, found itself with little need of a navy either to protect commerce, extend its territory, or defend itself.

The largest sea power at the time was the North African city of Carthage, in modern Tunisia. As the commercial capital of the Mediterranean, Carthage controlled ports throughout the western half of the sea, in Spain, northern Africa, Sardinia, and Sicily, and supplied the trading needs of at least 5 million people.

Rome and Carthage were able to coexist peacefully at first. Treaties kept Roman ships away from Carthaginian territories. In return, the Carthaginians promised not to attack Italy. Control of Sicily, however, would soon become an issue.

In 281 B.C., King Pyrrhus of Epirus attacked southern Italy. The Romans sent an army to defeat him and gained control over this Greek-speaking region as a result. Because the culture of southern Italy was based more on seafaring than that of Rome, the Romans soon realized that they would need to take a greater interest in naval security.

Meanwhile, the Carthaginians were engaged in a struggle over the fertile farmlands in Sicily. Their opponent, King Hiero of Syracuse, tried to bolster his position on the island by recapturing the important port city of Messana from a band of mercenaries who had once served under the king. The mercenaries, called Mamertines, asked for aid from both the Carthaginians and the Romans now stationed at Rhegium, just across the strait. With the support of a popular referendum, Rome agreed to intervene in 264 B.C.

The Romans, still lacking a real navy, crossed the straits in makeshift boats and joined the mercenaries in driving out the "helping" Carthaginians, who had already garrisoned the city for themselves. In retaliation, Carthage formed an alliance with Hiero against the Romans. The Roman forces, however, were able to hold the city, defeat the Carthaginians, and force Hiero into an alliance with Rome. Encouraged by this success, the Roman Senate resolved to expel the Carthaginians from all of Sicily. To accomplish their objective, however, the Romans would have to create their first real navy. Construction of new ships began in earnest in 261.

Rome's existing fleet, such as it was, consisted of about 40 triremes (ships needing three rowers for each oar), some of which may have been supplied by her allies. The Senate commissioned 20 new triremes and 100 quinqueremes (with five men to an oar), giving the Romans a numerical superiority over the Carthaginians' 130 ships. The ancient historian Polybius records that this undertaking was completed in 60 days. W. L. Rodgers, a modern naval historian, estimated the manpower required to complete such a task on schedule:

> If we take it that the Roman ships averaged not over 120 tons and that, being built in haste of green timber, they were not so well built as they might be and that in consequence they only called for 80 days' labor per ton, in the forest as well as in the dockyards, it follows that about 165 woodcutters, carpenters, and metal workers must have been employed on each of these ships, in order to complete the task in 60 days, or 20,000 men in all.[20]

The wars with Carthage lasted nearly 100 years. The first major battle was fought near Ecnomus in 256 B.C. Skirmishes and minor battles caused losses on both sides, but neither could win a decisive victory, and both continued building new ships to make up for the losses. Finally, a huge naval fight decided the issue: The Romans were victorious, sinking 64 of the Carthaginians' ships while losing only 22 of their own. Though many of the most famous battles of the Punic Wars were waged on land, the Romans still needed to maintain a substantial fleet to transport troops, disrupt the movements of the Carthaginians, and combat the enemy at sea whenever opportunities presented themselves.

After the Second Punic War, Rome's navy stayed active by aiding its allies in the Macedonian Wars. With the defeat of Antiochus in 190, however, the Romans eliminated their last major threat at sea, and the navy played a relatively

Though the navy had only a small role in the ultimate defeat of Carthage, the Punic Wars helped establish Rome as a formidable sea power. This naval equipment and training proved valuable as a precursor to the Battle of Actium.

minor role in the ultimate defeat of Carthage in 146. In fact, for the next 100 years, the fleet fell into something of a decline. Only in the middle of the first century B.C. would Rome's once-mighty navy regain its former strength when Julius Caesar built up the fleet for his campaigns in Gaul, Britain, Spain, and Africa.

THE SHIPS AT ACTIUM

Although Julius Caesar had left behind a capable navy, much of it had fallen under the command of Sextus

Pompeius. In order to combat this rival, Octavian and Agrippa had to build up a fleet of their own. Thus, before Octavian began his campaign against Antony, he already had an able fighting force at his disposal, for many of these ships survived and were available for use at Actium. Nevertheless, he needed an even bigger fleet if he hoped to be successful against the combined forces of Antony and Cleopatra.

According to Rodgers, the preexisting ships, which were a bit smaller than the ones Octavian would later have made for Actium, were probably about 105 feet long and 16.5 feet wide with a displacement of 81 tons.[21] Although the ships were equipped with sails, their primary means of propulsion, especially in battle, was the team of 108 rowers who sat in two tiers below the deck. The rowers on the lower tier, 18 to a side, each worked a shorter oar, while the rowers on the top tier sat in pairs with the two men working a single oar, again 18 to a side. These rowers were well trained and paid for their work; they were not slaves as often portrayed in the movies. Powered by rowers alone, the ship could achieve an attack speed of 7.3 knots and a cruising speed of 4.8 knots. The ship was maneuvered by the rowers, the sails (if used), and the two large rudders, one on each side of the stern. About 25 sailors were required to keep the boat in operation.

The weapons on Agrippa's triremes consisted chiefly of a ram on the bow and 60 soldiers standing on the edge of the deck. It is thought that these vessels also had platforms on each side extending over the oars but slightly below deck level. Thus, the soldiers on deck could throw their javelins over the heads of those standing on the platforms. At each end of the ship there was also a tower from which weapons could be deployed. We are fortunate to have a flat-relief sculpture depicting one of these ships. It is now housed in the Vatican Museum.

The Actian
Campaign

The Battle of Actium was seen as more than simply a naval battle in the strait of the Ambracian Gulf. It also posed Octavian against Antony, West against East, Roman sensibility against Egyptian licentiousness. Whoever or whichever won the battle, won control of the entire Roman Empire.

FINAL PREPARATIONS: 32–31 B.C.

By the end of 32, Antony's forces had taken position in the harbor of Actium, "a place sacred to Apollo and situated in front of the mouth of the strait leading into the Ambracian Gulf opposite the harbors of Nicopolis,"[22] wrote ancient historian Cassius Dio. Antony knew he had little chance in Italy, which was decisively controlled by Octavian, but in the East, things might be different. Although Octavian would be aided by Agrippa, Antony was clearly a more skilled and experienced commander than his younger triumviral colleague. He hoped that advantage would be enough.

The approach to Actium was dotted with harbors where ships

could be stationed to attack the approaching Octavian while his vessels were burdened with troops and supplies. In this state, configured for transport rather than combat, they were less maneuverable and more vulnerable to attack. Furthermore, because Octavian's ships were smaller, lighter, and faster when prepared for a fight, catching them by surprise on the way in provided Antony with the best prospect of success. Finally, since Antony had more ships (500 to Octavian's 400 or so, when the campaign began) and more men (100,000 to Octavian's 80,000), he could scatter them to harass Octavian's fleet yet still maintain an effective battle force at Actium itself.

During the winter of 32–31, Antony was camped at Patrae while Octavian sailed from Brundisium to Corcyra. All the while, both sides spent the winter spying upon and annoying each other. Octavian planned to move toward Actium as early as possible, hoping to turn the tables on Marc Antony and catch him by surprise, but a storm caused Octavian to withdraw. Agrippa, meanwhile, was more successful, capturing Methone and Corcyra over the objections of Antony's soldiers stationed nearby. For reasons that remain unsatisfactorily explained, Antony seems to have all but ignored Octavian's movements during these skirmishes with Agrippa. Indeed, if the young Caesar met with any significant resistance, no record of it has survived.[23] Octavian chose a spot just north of Corcyra for his camp and soon advanced to Actium, where he occupied the hill of Mikalitzi — good ground to hold.

It can be argued that the events of the winter of 32–31 effectively decided the battle fought later that summer. Since Octavian's fleet had made it to Actium intact, and since Antony's fleet had already suffered some losses, the tide was turning in Octavian's favor. Of course, Octavian would still have to perform well in a major battle, but he probably would have had no chance if Antony had prevailed in these initial skirmishes.

Once Octavian made it to Actium, it was possible for him to take up an advantageous position there. Actium itself is a promontory situated at the mouth of a narrow inlet or strait leading into the Ambracian Gulf. Antony moored his ships along both sides of this long strait, built towers on both sides of the mouth, and stationed guard ships so that other vessels could safely come and go at will. He camped on a plain on the far side of the strait, but quarters were tight and water was scarce. Under these conditions and in the summer heat, good sanitation was difficult to maintain, so his men were ravaged by disease. Octavian's men were more fortunate. Camped on a hill near Nicopolis, they could view both land and sea. Friendly ships in the gulf blockaded Antony's fleet while allowing fresh water and supplies to reach the men. For several days, Octavian offered battle, but Antony did not accept.

During this time, Agrippa was achieving further victories. First he captured Leucas and Patrae, where Antony had spent the winter. Then Gnaeus Domitius defected from Antony to Octavian, a defection that spurred others to do the same. Perhaps urged on by the unrest in Antony's camp and the victories of Agrippa, Octavian's advance guard, led by Marcus Titius and Statilius Taurus, made a successful assault on Antony's cavalry.

The day held one minor piece of good fortune for Antony. While Agrippa was away with the main fleet, Sosius, one of Antony's admirals, spotted Statilius Taurus nearby. Separated from Agrippa, Statilius was vulnerable, and Sosius made a predawn surprise attack under the cover of a thick mist. The attack scattered Statilius's fleet, but Sosius was never able to capture his opponent because Agrippa arrived and cut off his pursuit. Thus, the only potentially positive development for Antony came to nothing.

As the military situation was turning to favor Octavian, political advantage followed. Antony's royal allies in the region were either defeated in battle, killed, or defecting to Octavian. Even some of Antony's Roman commanders were switching sides, hoping to ally themselves with the man who increasingly looked like the winner.

By September of 31, Antony's prospects of success had become as bleak as they were promising just a few months before. What did he intend to do? The ancient historian Dio suggests that Antony had no desire to fight a decisive battle at Actium but rather wanted to break through Octavian's blockade and sail to Egypt. The most compelling evidence for such a view is the presence of two items carried by his fleet: his treasure and sails, neither of which would have typically been found on warships intent on battle. Others have concluded, usually on the basis of an analysis of the actual battle, that Antony intended to fight to win. More plausible is the view, widely held by historians today, that Antony was prepared for either contingency. Scholars such as W.W. Tarn emphasized the battle: Antony was intent on victory but would withdraw to Egypt if there was no hope of success.[24] Other authorities such as J. Kromayer emphasized the flight: He planned to break out to Egypt but was willing to stay and fight if he got lucky and the battle went well.[25] Unfortunately, Antony's true motives are forever lost to us.

ACTIUM

Although the Battle of Actium is widely regarded as one of the most important naval battles in Roman history, few details of the fighting are known for sure.

There are several accounts of the battle by ancient historians, and several tantalizing clues are offered by the art and literature of the period, but the contemporary evidence is sometimes in conflict and often unreliable. As the distinguished twentieth-century historian Sir Ronald Syme bluntly put it, "The true story is gone beyond recall."[26] What follows, then, is at best a tentative and partial reconstruction of events, a theory of what might have happened, based on the best guesses of generations of scholars.

A charming, and probably false, story about Octavian represents in many ways the character of much ancient writing on Actium with its pro-Octavian slant (for historical writing tends to favor the winner) and its fondness for far-fetched tales and incredible omens. As Octavian was making his way from camp to the ships on the morning of battle, he encountered a man and his donkey. When asked to identify himself, the man replied, "My name is Eutychus (Good Fortune) and that of my ass is Nicon (Victory)." Octavian relayed the story to his men before they set sail to meet Antony, and he later erected a statue of the man and his donkey on the spot of the encounter. Octavian may never have met the "Good Fortune" and "Victory" of the story, but even if the meeting never occurred, there is no reason to suspect that Octavian would not have fabricated such a story in an effort to inspire his men.

Antony, for his part, had probably planned to engage on August 29, but bad weather forced a delay. On September 2, under clear skies and calm winds, both fleets lined up for battle.

The precise size of the forces present at the battle is uncertain, especially since Antony had lost men to disease during the previous months. Nevertheless, reasonably good estimates are possible. Octavian's ship strength may be reliably set at over 400. The number of ships under Antony's command is somewhat more controversial, but 400 is a reasonable guess, since he had seven squadrons of 60 ships each, but not all squadrons were operating at full strength. Some authorities give smaller numbers on both sides, but the discrepancy is likely explained by the fact that most of the fighting took place at the northern end of the line, thus involving few ships in the actual battle.

Antony's seven squadrons were deployed in three units of two, with Cleopatra's squadron, the seventh, serving as rear guard. In the Macedonian tradition, to which Cleopatra belonged, the rear guard was the position of honor for elite troops, not a cowardly position of safety, as has often been said. The two squadrons of the left were commanded by Sosius, the center was held by Insteius and Marcus Octavius (not to be confused with Octavian), and Antony traveled with Publicola, the commander of the right, or northern, wing. This right flank, consisting of just under 120 ships, formed a line of about 5,000 yards, with 40 to 50 yards separating each ship,[27] according to W.L. Rodgers.

Agrippa's line was longer, perhaps 8,000 yards wide and with as many as 260 ships. This longer line was necessary because it was farther out to sea and formed a wide arc around the mouth of the harbor so as not to be outflanked. Octavian traveled with the right wing, which was commanded by Lurius, and Arruntius held the center. The entire western line positioned itself about 1,600 yards from the opposing navy.

The position of the commanders-in-chief on the right flanks was customary among the Romans, who considered it the place of honor. At Actium, this custom worked to the advantage of both sides. Antony, whose position was to the north, could direct the effort to get around the back of, or

Victory in such a naval battle depended on the number of ships on each side, the strength of the rowers below deck, the bravery of the soldiers on deck, and the strategy of the commanders observing from the right flanks.

outflank, his adversary and could oversee the difficult maneuver of turning both lines with the wind that was expected out of the north-northwest later that afternoon. His strategy was to use the wind to push the enemy fleet toward the shore, where it could be besieged from sea and land. With Octavian holding the southern end of the line, the crucial left flank remained for Agrippa, whose naval skill and expertise would be needed to prevent Antony from accomplishing his objective—an objective that Agrippa must have foreseen.

Although the ships probably sailed into formation around dawn, there was little action until midday, with both sides delaying the assault to make it coincide with the shifting afternoon winds.

Antony made the first move and advanced against Agrippa. At the opposite end of the line, Sosius also moved against Lurius and Octavian, who withdrew, perhaps with the intention of pulling Sosius away from the shore and then circling around to attack him from the rear. Agrippa employed a different tactic and moved quickly to the north in an effort to outflank Antony, who was also moving northward with the same objective.

This parallel northern movement did not take place without conflict, but the two sides employed somewhat different combat tactics. Cassius Dio described the contrast:

> Caesar's followers, having smaller and swifter ships, would dash forward and ram the enemy, being armored on all sides to avoid receiving damage. If they sank a vessel, well and good; if not, they would back water before coming to grips, and would either ram the same vessels suddenly again, or would let those go and turn their attention to others.
>
> The enemy, on the other hand, tried to hit the approaching ships with dense showers of stones and arrows and to cast iron grapnels upon their assailants. And in case they could reach them they got the better of it, but if they missed, their own boats would be pierced and would sink. . . .[28]

Because Antony and Publicola had fewer ships, the flanking maneuver drew more of their ships away from the center. Arruntius seized the opportunity and attacked. Meanwhile, the afternoon winds had arrived, and Cleopatra, finding an opening in the now turbulent and scattered center, set sail. Antony left his flagship in favor of a smaller vessel and joined Cleopatra.

It is difficult to know whether this "escape" was the culmination of a brilliantly planned and perfectly executed operation or whether it was an improvised withdrawal from a losing battle. Indeed, it is entirely possible that Cleopatra's advance was actually an offensive gesture, a move to attack (at least at first) rather than flee. Although Octavian's forces did ultimately get the better of things after Antony and Cleopatra left, it is similarly difficult to pinpoint the reasons for such success. Had Octavian and Agrippa already won the contest through superior fighting before Antony and Cleopatra withdrew, or had the very act of withdrawal turned the tide by provoking defections and dispirited fighting? The evidence allows for no clear conclusion.

The end result, however, is that Antony and Cleopatra escaped to Egypt with some of their ships—perhaps about 40 but certainly no more than 100.[29] By the late afternoon, the Battle of Actium had ended, and Agrippa had captured some 300 ships, if the calculations of ancient historian Plutarch are to be believed. The land forces, unable to work out any other arrangement, surrendered to Octavian, who found it politically advantageous to be merciful.

Sir Ronald Syme wrote that, although Octavian would later endow Actium with "august dimensions and intense emotional colors" befitting "a great naval battle,"[30] it was, in fact, something of a disappointment—so much so that even usually sober historians have given it the adjectives "lame"[31] and "shabby."[32] In military terms, Octavian had won, but Antony and Cleopatra had escaped, which was, in a sense, a victory for them and an embarrassment for Octavian. It would not be long, however, before the lovers would meet their end in Egypt.

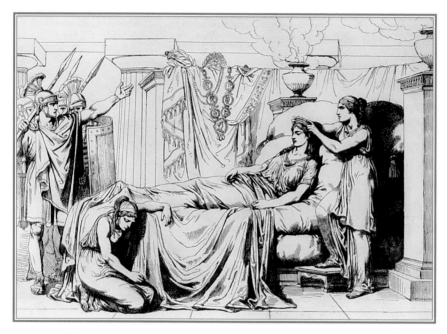

Antony and Cleopatra lost the Battle of Actium and quickly returned to Alexandria. In Roman public opinion, Antony's defeat proved true Octavian's claims of superiority, and Octavian enjoyed a triumphal return home. No such rejoicing awaited Antony and Cleopatra in Egypt, however.

ALEXANDRIA

Although Octavian's ships were lighter and faster than Antony's, they lacked the sails of their fleeing adversary, so there would have been little point in pursuit, even if the vessels remaining at Actium could have been defeated quickly. Besides, there would be time for an Egyptian campaign soon enough. First, however, Octavian needed to subdue the Eastern provinces previously controlled by Antony, a task that proved surprisingly easy, for most of Antony's legions had been gathered at Actium or were dispatched to Egypt to protect Cleopatra's interests while she was away.

Public opinion in Italy, already on Octavian's side, only increased with Antony's flight into Egypt. Nevertheless, the 30s had been a turbulent decade of civil wars, and there were still some troubles at home. Of particular concern was the ever-increasing number of veterans returning to Rome and demanding land, which was in short supply. Octavian could not risk seizing land for fear of increased civil strife, so he decided to buy it. The fact that he didn't actually have the funds was of no consequence. Soon enough the riches of the East—Antony's treasure and, more importantly, Cleopatra's—would be his.

With the provinces under control by the end of 31, Octavian returned briefly to Rome to settle his affairs. Because he and his supporters had successfully mobilized public opinion against Antony and Cleopatra, it came as no surprise to Octavian that he should receive a hero's welcome. The outpouring of support may well have been genuine, but partisan squabbling would have served no purpose, and the few pockets of resistance that still existed made little difference. The matter was settled, and Octavian was master of Rome.

In early 30, he set out for Egypt, sailing first to the Ionian coast and then marching his troops by land toward Alexandria. Meanwhile, Cornelius Gallus would make a western approach to support the attack. The journey would take time, and Octavian wanted to ensure that Cleopatra did not squander or destroy the riches he needed in Rome. He therefore engaged the queen in secret negotiations, perhaps offering to spare her life in exchange for Antony's or perhaps suggesting that he might allow the Ptolemies to rule as Roman clients. The negotiations came to nothing, however, and it is doubtful that they were ever meant to be anything more than delaying tactics on Octavian's part as he made his way to Egypt.

On July 31, the eve of Octavian's planned attack, the general enacted an old Roman rite known as the evocation, or "calling out," of the foreign enemy's gods, entreating them to support the Romans, who would honor them if victorious. Plutarch describes the event:

> During this night, it is said, about the middle of it, while the city was quiet and depressed through fear and expectation of what was coming, suddenly certain harmonious sounds from all sorts of instruments were heard, and the shouting of a throng, accompanied by cries of Bacchic revelry and satyric leapings, as if a troop of revelers, making a great tumult, were going forth from the city.[33]

There was great symbolic significance in the act. According to historian Macrobius, the same rite was "probably enacted before the fall of Carthage," another African kingdom defeated by the Romans.[34] Further, Antony had been portraying himself as Dionysus (or the Egyptian god Osiris), so the rite may have also symbolized the abandonment of his divine support. As Plutarch put it, "The god to whom Antony always most likened and attached himself was now deserting him."[35]

The actual fighting at Alexandria on August 1 did not amount to much. Antony's fleet surrendered to Octavian without hostilities, and the cavalry immediately followed suit. When he saw that his infantry would not be successful, Antony sought refuge within the city and was convinced that Cleopatra had betrayed him. No doubt there was a bit more to the siege than the ancient sources record (Plutarch, for instance, devotes barely a line to it), but they were perhaps understandably eager to move on to the spectacular suicides of Antony and Cleopatra.

Antony's end, in Plutarch's account, had all the makings of a good opera plot, and Shakespeare later recognized its dramatic possibilities. When Cleopatra realized that Antony had lost the battle, Plutarch wrote that she locked herself inside her tomb and sent messengers to inform

Antony of her death. Antony, believing this false report, resolved to take his own life, saying, "O Cleopatra, I am not grieved to be bereft of thee, for I shall straight-way join you; but I am grieved that such an imperator as I am has been found to be inferior to a woman in courage."[36] He then ordered his slave Eros to stab him with a dagger, but the slave killed himself instead. "Well done, Eros!" said Antony. "You teach me what I must do,"[37] whereupon Antony stabbed himself in the belly.

The wound was not immediately fatal, however. In his weakened state, Antony begged those around him to finish him off, but they all fled. Soon Cleopatra learned that her lover was alive, and she ordered him to be brought to her tomb. In lamentation, the queen tore her garments and smeared her body with Antony's blood, hailing him as "master, husband, and imperator."[38] Antony, in turn, advised Cleopatra to look to her own safety and not to lament his fate but to be happy in his triumphs, for "he had become the most illustrious of men, had won greatest power, and now had been not ignobly conquered, a Roman by a Roman."[39]

In Act IV of *Antony and Cleopatra*, Shakespeare drama-tized the final moments shared by the lovers, with words reminiscent of Thomas North's 1579 translation of Plutarch, upon which he relied:

Antony: The miserable change now at my end
          Lament nor sorrow at; but please your thoughts
          In feeding them with those my former fortunes
          Wherein I liv'd, the greatest prince o' th' world,
          The noblest; and do now not basely die,
          Not cowardly put off my helmet to
          My countryman,—a Roman by a Roman
          Valiantly vanquish'd. Now my spirit is going;
          I can no more.

Cleopatra: Noblest of men, woo't die?
Hast thou no care of me? Shall I abide
In this dull world, which in thy absence is
No better than a sty? O, see, my women,
The crown o' the earth doth melt. My lord!
O, wither'd is the garland of the war,
The soldier's pole is fall'n: young boys and girls
Are level now with men; the odds is gone,
And there is nothing left remarkable
Beneath the visiting moon.[40]

Antony was dead, and Octavian quickly saw to the death of Antony's son Antyllus. He also hunted down the few remaining conspirators who had sought refuge in Egypt after his great-uncle's murder. Cleopatra, fearing for

Shakespeare's Roman Plays

William Shakespeare (1564–1616), widely considered the greatest poet of the English language, was fascinated by ancient Rome and wrote four plays on Roman topics. Set in the late days of the Roman Empire, *Titus Andronicus* (written in 1594) depicts the violent hatred between the sadistic general Titus and Tamora, the captured queen of the Goths, who spend the play trying to avenge each other's escalating acts of brutality. *Julius Caesar* (1599) follows Brutus and Cassius from their initial plot to kill the dictator, through the assassination and funeral of Caesar, up to their defeat at Philippi. *Antony and Cleopatra* (1608) chronicles the lovers' decadent life in Egypt, their defeat at the Battle of Actium, and their suicides in Alexandria. *Coriolanus*, probably written after *Antony and Cleopatra* in 1608, is set in the early days of the Roman Republic (about 490 B.C.) and treats a classic Roman subject: the class struggle between patricians and plebeians. Even Shakespeare's non-Roman plays frequently allude to classical stories, and his *Romeo and Juliet* is strongly reminiscent of the myth of Pyramus and Thisbe, as told by the Roman poet Ovid.

Caesarion, her illegitimate son by Julius Caesar, sent the boy to India. Octavian, however, probably did not plan to kill Caesarion—at least not yet—and he spared Cleopatra's other children, perhaps with the intention of using them to help prevent the queen's suicide. Indeed, Octavian very much wanted Cleopatra to remain alive. She had been the centerpiece of his propaganda campaign against Antony and was therefore the ultimate symbol of victory. Marching the captured queen through the streets of Rome as part of his triumphal parade would delight the masses, and Octavian, ever the politician, craved such affirmation.

Such an ending was not to be. Cleopatra must have realized Octavian's intentions and was unwilling to face the humiliation, so she planned her own suicide. At first she tried to stab herself, but Proculeius, a lieutenant of Octavian, snatched the dagger from her hands. He then increased the guards and put Cleopatra under the ancient equivalent of a "suicide watch."

On the ninth day of her captivity, Cleopatra was brought a basket of figs after a bath. Upon removing some of the figs, the queen uncovered a snake, or asp, in the basket. She offered her arm, not her breast as is popularly supposed. The snake bit it, and the queen succumbed to the poison.

This story of Cleopatra's death may be fictional, and even the ancients offered conflicting accounts. Some believed that the snakebite was accidental, while others suggested that Cleopatra arranged for the snake to be brought to her. Some even shed doubt on the very existence of the asp. Plutarch acknowledged reports that Cleopatra had poison hidden in a hollow comb, and he is forced to admit that "the truth of the matter no one knows."[41]

Although Cleopatra had frustrated Octavian's plans for a grand triumph, in Plutarch's account, Octavian

Cleopatra allegedly committed suicide in 30 B.C. Thus, her final role in world history was as a tragic figure. Poets and historians have repeatedly examined her cunning, beauty, and mystery.

nevertheless "admired her lofty spirit"[42] and allowed for her to receive a royal burial with Marc Antony at her side as he had been for the last 14 years. Octavian also spared all of Cleopatra's children except Caesarion, and all of Antony's except Antyllus, whom he had already killed. He then set about removing all the statues of Antony from Egypt, and he would have removed Cleopatra's as well, but, always in need of money, he accepted a bribe of 2000 talents (coins) to leave them standing.

The vast treasures of Egypt now belonged to Octavian alone. Although the African kingdom officially became part of the Roman Empire, Octavian treated it as his own special possession. Gaius Cornelius Gallus, a close friend and the general who supported Octavian's final battle at Alexandria, become its first governor.

For the rest of 30, Octavian traveled through the Eastern provinces, cementing alliances with local leaders and bolstering his power in the region before returning to Rome. On August 13, 29 B.C., he entered the capital city to lavish celebrations of his conquests. After decades of civil war, Julius Caesar's heir was now the sole ruler of the Roman world. Fate would give him over 40 years in which to build a legacy for the victory he won at Actium.

The victories of Octavian (shown here in profile) earned him several promotions, and he became known as "Augustus," Princeps, holder of the Tribunician Power, and eventually, emperor. All of this was just the beginning of his career; he ruled for more than 40 years after winning the Battle of Actium.

The Age of Augustus

THE HOMECOMING

The homecoming of Octavian in the summer of 29 was marked by both symbolic pomp and substantive political activity, all of which served to reinforce the authority of the Actian victor.

His triumphal procession lasted for three days. The first day was devoted to his Illyrian campaign of 34, an old and relatively minor success that had already been honored years ago but which was now "remembered with advantages" (as Shakespeare's Henry V would say). Historian R.A. Gurval told how celebrations of the Battle of Actium itself occurred on August 14, an unprecedented event, for never before had a single battle received a full and formal triumph.[43] Octavian, however, used the occasion less to glorify himself than to honor the allies who assisted him and to draw attention away from the fact that the battle was essentially part of a civil war.[44] Indeed, the focus of the climactic third day was the defeat of Cleopatra, a foreign enemy whose riches Octavian the Imperator paraded through the streets of Rome. The three-day triumph was an extravagantly expensive affair, but the wealth of Egypt was substantial—so great, in fact, that Octavian gave a large sum (400 sesterces apiece) directly to the people.

The remaining months of 29 were also filled with administrative and legislative accomplishments. First, Octavian closed the Temple of Janus, to signal the official end of war. Then he scaled back the army and colonized his veterans, buying land for them as needed. This action was an astute political move on Octavian's part. Maintaining a large standing army might have implied a desire to hunt down Antony's old supporters and thus to extend the civil wars. By disbanding the army, Octavian signaled instead a return to normalcy and gave the impression that his own power was so secure that such military might was unnecessary. Next, Octavian ordered a long-overdue census, or counting of the people, reduced the number of senators, and reorganized the Senate with himself as *Princeps Senatus*, or "First Citizen of the Senate." To carry out all these initiatives, Octavian assumed the consulship again in 28 and remained in Rome for the entire year.

Octavian, the Princeps, was firmly in control but also careful always to work within a constitutional framework. Fearing that the fate of Julius Caesar might await him if he overreached, Octavian was at pains to be seen as a restorer of the Republic, although restorer of "constitutional government" or even "constitutional monarchy" might be a fairer label,[45] according to Scullard. In 27, Octavian surrendered all his own territorial possessions to the Senate, which immediately placed him in charge of most of them. It also conferred upon him the title of "Augustus."

THE YEAR 23

In 25, Augustus arranged the marriage of his daughter Julia to his nephew Marcellus. Young Marcellus was a leader of extraordinary promise, having served as quaestor and ready to stand for an aedileship in 23. It is possible that Augustus was already concerned with providing for his succession, for he was prone to illness and may not have expected to live a long life.

Those concerns took on new urgency in the summer of 23, when Augustus became deathly sick. After a series of bizarre cold-water treatments supervised by Antonius Musa, his Greek doctor, Augustus recovered, but Marcellus died that fall. Many in Rome felt that the loss was devastating, and the poet Virgil wrote of Marcellus,

> Never will any boy of Ilian race
> Exalt his Latin forefathers with promise
> Equal to his; never will Romulus' land
> Take pride like this in any of her sons.
> Weep for his faithful heart, his old-world honor,
> His sword arm never beaten down! No enemy
> Could have come through a clash with him unhurt,
> Whether this soldier went on foot or rode,
> Digging his spurs into a lathered mount.[46]

Soon after Marcellus's death, Augustus placed Julia in the

hands of his friend and military ally Agrippa. They would be married in 21.

The year 23 was significant for other reasons as well. A conspiracy to restore the Republic was afoot, and Augustus's co-consul, Fannius Caepio, was implicated in the plot. Although it is unlikely that the conspiracy had any real chance of success, it nevertheless revealed that republican sentiments had not disappeared completely.

After the conspirators were executed, Augustus decided to resign his consulship, perhaps to avoid the perception that he was offending Roman tradition by holding the consulship for too many years in a row. What may have seemed like a prorepublican move, however, actually turned out to increase the power of the Princeps, for the Senate quickly expanded his official responsibilities to make up for the loss of consular authority. First, the senators increased his *imperium*, or "power of command," to make it greater than that of any other proconsul. Second, the imperium would be valid throughout the empire, not just in the provinces that were already officially under his control. Finally, Augustus received the Tribunician Power, which made him the most powerful man in Rome itself. Thus, he now had full constitutional authority to command armies, implement policies, and override the actions of other officials. In short, the Princeps was now a full-fledged emperor. Though Augustus would seek the consulship several more times throughout his reign, he did not need the office to carry out his will. He was already the legal ruler of the Roman world.

A CHANGING SOCIETY

Augustus spent the next three years in the East, and he counted among his greatest diplomatic achievements the recovery of the Roman standards from the Parthians,

The Age of Augustus that followed the Battle of Actium was marked by diplomatic, judicial, and moral accomplishments. Municipal building projects and a flourishing literature signified improvements in the more aesthetic aspects of Roman society.

long-time enemies of Rome. Indeed, this event is the central scene on the breastplate worn by the emperor in the famous sculpture, *Augustus of Prima Porta*.

The Princeps went abroad again from 16–13 for a campaign in Gaul. Upon his return he erected the *Ara Pacis Augustae*, or "Augustus's Altar of Peace," in the Campus Martius as a celebration of the *Pax Romana* ("Roman Peace"), which the empire now enjoyed. From 13 on, the emperor spent most of his reign in Rome, sending Agrippa or other deputies on foreign missions. From the capital he could concentrate on the domestic agenda that would characterize his principate perhaps even more than his military successes.

Almost all of the legal measures instituted by Augustus had the ostensible purpose of making Rome a more moral state. He tightened the laws against bribery and corruption, standardized the administration of justice in the provinces, and initiated an appeals process in which the emperor would have the final say. Augustus also sought to improve personal morality and promote the traditional Roman family. At his urging, the Popular Assembly ratified a series of *Leges Juliae*, or "Julian Laws," which regulated marriage and divorce and criminalized adultery. Indeed, Augustus's daughter Julia was exiled for violating these laws. The emperor's own indiscretions, however, went unchecked.

As a financial manager, Augustus was quite successful. He saw to it that the provinces were all self financing, for they would neither send tribute to Rome nor receive funds from the central government to carry out their affairs. The principal sources of revenue, besides the profits of conquest, were sales and death taxes. Although the Senate was officially in charge of the money supply, Augustus's control of gold and silver mines throughout the empire afforded him great fiscal authority. The imperial mint located in Gaul, which Augustus directed, easily supplanted the Senate-run mint in Rome, and coins bearing the emperor's likeness far outnumbered Senate-minted coins.

Augustus made the famous claim that he had found Rome brick and left it marble. Although poverty was an undeniably prevalent component of urban life, it existed beside some of the greatest public building projects of the ancient world. The Princeps completely rebuilt the Forum, including a new temple to Mars the Avenger. Office buildings, storefronts, and warehouses provided for the practical needs of city living. Roads, bridges, and aqueducts were built, enlarged, and maintained, and an elaborate system of plumbing and sewage kept opulent bath houses in operation, while libraries and theaters met the cultural needs of Roman citizens.

Literature flourished during the Augustan Age. The emperor himself, along with his friend Maecenas, was a great patron of the arts, and commissioned poetry from Horace and Virgil and a history of Rome from Livy. Though many modern writers glibly criticize these three authors for spreading pro-Augustan propaganda, the ancient writers' work in fact displays great sophistication and subtlety, and Augustus seems to have had a genuine appreciation for fine literature. The one blemish in his record as a supporter of the arts is the exile of the poet Ovid for an unknown indiscretion, possibly involving the emperor's granddaughter.

The greatest literary achievement of the Augustan Age is Virgil's *Aeneid*, an epic poem about the hero Aeneas who sailed from Troy to Italy in order to found a new nation that would become the Roman Empire. Because Augustus claimed to be descended from Aeneas, the *Aeneid* is often interpreted as a poem that praises the emperor through the glory of his ancestors. Indeed, Virgil explicitly mentions Augustus himself:

> This is the man, this one,
> Of whom so often you have heard the promise,
> Caesar Augustus, son of the deified,
> Who shall bring once again an Age of Gold
> To Latium, to the land where Saturn reigned
> In early times. He will extend his power
> Beyond the Garamants and Indians,
> Over far territories north and south
> Of the zodiacal stars, the solar way,
> Where Atlas, heaven-bearing, on his shoulder
> Turns the night-sphere, studded with burning stars.[47]

Although some modern readers have found parts of the *Aeneid* to be critical of Augustus, the emperor does not seem to have been put off by anything he read. Virgil died before he could finish revising the poem, and legend has it that the poet ordered his creation to be burned, but Augustus intervened and saved the manuscript from the flames. If true, Augustus's rescue of the *Aeneid* would be as enduring an accomplishment as any.

DEATH AND LEGACY

Because Augustus had no direct male heir, he knew that succession would be an issue. The premature death of Marcellus had prevented the young man from giving Julia a son, and Julia's sons from her marriage to Agrippa had already died. The only other close relatives were Drusus and Tiberius, the sons of his wife, Livia, from her previous marriage to Tiberius Claudius Nero. Since Drusus was also already dead, there was nobody left but Tiberius, whom Augustus did not particularly like. Nevertheless, he promptly adopted his stepson in A.D. 4 after the death of Gaius Caesar, Julia's last surviving male child.

Augustus himself died on August 19, A.D. 14, leaving Tiberius to succeed him. The funeral was predictably lavish, and mourners paraded the emperor's body to the Campus Martius, where it was cremated. Tiberius and his son Drusus delivered funeral orations. Within a month, the Senate deified Augustus, declaring that he had been a god, just as it had deified Julius Caesar.

Even in death, the Princeps continued to exert his influence. Early in his reign, Augustus realized that his hold on power came not just from military might or the backing of the Senate. It came from his own accomplishments and the tangible benefits afforded to

Augustus died in A.D. 14 and is buried in this mausoleum in Rome. He had no direct male heir; therefore his death caused just as much political upheaval as Caesar's death had done 58 years earlier.

the Roman people. Peace, prosperity, grand public works, and a flowering of the arts were all magnificent contributions, but the emperor was wise never to underestimate the power of money. Cash disbursements occurred several times during his reign, and in his will Augustus provided even more money: 43 million sesterces for the people of Rome. In addition, according to Southern, 1,000 sesterces went to each praetorian, 500 to each of his urban troops, and 300 to each of his legionaries.[48]

The 44-year reign of Gaius Julius Caesar Octavianus, Augustus, Imperator, and Princeps had its share of triumphs and defeats, virtues and vices. It was an era of unparalleled peace, but that peace had come only after brutal war and brought with it a certain loss of liberty and democracy. Nevertheless, the improvements in the daily lives of most Romans living under Augustus have

The Ara Pacis

Augustus's return from Gaul in the year 13 B.C. marked the completion of his efforts to unite all corners of the empire under his command. In return for its unquestioned allegiance to Augustus, the Mediterranean world enjoyed protection from foreign aggression, freedom from civil war, and a period of stability known as the *Pax Augusta*, or "peace of Augustus." In his *Res Gestae Divi Augusti* (*The Accomplishments of the Divine Augustus*), the emperor explained how the Senate honored him for bringing peace to Rome:

> When I returned from Spain and Gaul, in the consulship of Tiberius Nero and Publius Quintilius, after successful operations in those provinces, the Senate voted in honour of my return the consecration of an altar to Pax Augusta in the Campus Martius, and on this altar it ordered the magistrates and priests and Vestal virgins to make annual sacrifice.*

The *Ara Pacis*, or "altar of peace," was made out of Parian marble and decorated with historical and mythological scenes that glorified Rome. In addition, Augustus's *Res Gestae* were inscribed on the altar as a reminder of how peace had been achieved. Erected on the Via Flaminia, the altar received its formal consecration on January 30, 9 B.C. and remained in active use for many years.

* *Source*: Augustus, *Res Gestae.* tr. Frederick W. Shipley, Cambridge: Harvard University Press, 1992, p. 365.

led the majority of modern historians to consider him, on balance, a successful leader. However the Augustan Principate is ultimately judged, one fact is difficult to deny: It established the model of imperial government that would endure unbroken for centuries and influence rulers even up to our own day.

Horace was one of many poets of the Augustan Age supported by Octavian. His excellent writings are understandably complimentary of his patron yet contain great wit and charm. Still, the "Cleopatra Ode" reveals sympathy for the fallen queen among heaping criticism.

Actium in Literature

The poets of the Augustan Age frequently alluded to the Battle of Actium in their works, sometimes at length. Because many of these poets were either directly or indirectly supported by Octavian-Augustus and Maecenas, it is often argued that the resulting poetry is little more than thinly veiled Augustan propaganda. In recent decades, however, literary critics and historians alike have found greater subtlety in the poetry of Actium and more ambiguous judgments about Augustus.

The closing pages of this volume will present a few of the poems of Horace and Virgil—arguably the two greatest poets of the day. Although each reader will have to make his or her own judgment about the depths of the poets' Augustan sympathies, few will be able to deny the power and beauty of the poems themselves.

HORACE

Quintus Horatius Flaccus, or "Horace," was born in the Apulian town of Venusia in 65 B.C. His father, although most likely a native Italian, had once been enslaved but eventually either won or bought his freedom and became a successful auctioneer. Horace studied in Rome and Athens before embarking on a career in public service, first in the military and then on the staff of a quaestor.

When Horace was about 20, he published his first collection of *Satires*. The strength of these satires caught the eye of Maecenas, a great patron of the arts and friend of Octavian, and a second book appeared five years later. About the same time, in 30 or 29, Horace produced a collection of lyric poems called *Epodes*. Written in the tradition of the Greek poets Archilochus and Hipponax, the *Epodes* were composed chiefly in iambic meters, and treated a variety of subjects, including the Battle of Actium, which occurred only a year or two before the collection was published.

Horace's greatest fame rests on his *Odes*, lyric poems in the grand style and in Greek meters. The first three books of the *Odes* he published in 23 B.C., with a final book to follow ten years later. Augustus is mentioned several times in the collection, and the next to last poem of the first book treats the death of Cleopatra after the Battle of Actium. Horace also gained fame as a literary critic who produced two books of *Epistles*, including his "Letter to the Pisones," commonly known as "The Art of Poetry."

The poetry of Horace is known for its linguistic sophistication, formal polish, and noble themes. Celebrated within his own lifetime, Horace remains one of the most admired figures in the history of Western poetry. His wit and charm, coupled with the dignity and refinement of his verse, have provided inspiration for poets throughout the last two millennia.

EPODE 1.9

Epode 1.9 holds a unique place among Actian poems because some historians have considered it a valuable source of information about the conduct of the battle. W.W. Tarn, for instance, gave the poem great weight in his reconstruction of Actium. On the other hand, we should be careful about expecting the poet and the historian to share similar aims, and *Epode 1.9* is perhaps better understood as one man's creative response to the battle rather than a literal account of its events.

The epode is addressed to Maecenas, with whom the speaker of the poem, conventionally understood to be Horace himself, wishes to celebrate Octavian's victory at Actium. Music, feasting, and choice Caecuban wine are to accompany the celebration, just as they did after Octavian's defeat of Sextus Pompeius at Naulochus.

The middle section of the poem was an attack on Marc Antony, calling him the unmanly pawn of Cleopatra:

> The Roman bears stakes and weapons at a woman's behest,
> and, a soldier, can bring himself to become the minion
> of withered eunuchs, while amid the soldiers' standards
> the sun shines on the shameful Egyptian pavilion.[49]

This portrayal of Antony is quite similar to Octavian's own characterizations of his rival, and Horace, perhaps anticipating that he would be called a mere mouthpiece of Octavian, predicts that posterity will deny the charges he has placed at Antony's feet.

As Horace goes on to describe the arrangement and movements of the fleet, cries of triumph punctuate his account. The Actian victory was favorably compared with other military successes, whereupon the poet called for more wine and concluded with the words, "'Tis sweet to banish anxious fear for Caesar's fortunes with Bacchus' mellow gift."[50]

THE CLEOPATRA ODE

Horace began his so-called "Cleopatra Ode" (*Odes 1.37*) on a note of celebration that echoes the Actium epode:

> Now is the time to drain the flowing bowl, now with unfettered foot to beat the ground with dancing, now with Salian feast to deck the couches of the gods, my comrades![51]

Cleopatra, a "frenzied queen . . . plotting ruin 'gainst the Capitol and destruction to the empire" and "a woman mad enough to nurse the wildest hopes and drunk with Fortune's favours," is dead,[52] wrote Horace.

For all the criticism of Cleopatra and for all the rejoicing at her defeat and death, however, Horace also betrays a certain sympathy for the queen. In lines that exaggerate the magnitude of her military defeat and accelerate Octavian's pursuit, Cleopatra is compared to a "gentle dove" followed by a hawk (Octavian) or a hare pursued by a hunter. Moreover, Horace sees her suicide not as a cowardly act but as a noble attempt to preserve her honor and deprive her adversary of his prize. He wrote,

> Yet she, seeking to die a nobler death, showed for the dagger's point no woman's fear, nor sought to win with her swift fleet some secret shore; she even dared to gaze with face serene upon the fallen palace; courageous,

too, to handle poisonous asps, that she might draw black venom to her heart, waxing bolder as she resolved to die; scorning, in sooth, the thought of being borne, a queen no longer, on hostile galleys to grace a glorious triumph—no craven woman she![53]

With these words, Horace thus expressed uncertainty about Actium. It was, to be sure, a triumph for Octavian, whose victory preserved the security of the Roman state. At the same time, however, a bold and noble leader was defeated that day, and she died an honorable death.

VIRGIL

Publius Vergilius Maro, or "Virgil," was born in Mantua in 70 B.C. during the first consulship of Pompey and Crassus. He came of age during the civil wars and attracted the attention of a man named Pollio, who became his first patron. According to ancient sources, Virgil lost his family farm in the land confiscations of the 40s that were intended to provide settlements for the veterans of Philippi. Through influential connections, and possibly with the intervention of Octavian himself, Virgil got his farm back but never forgot the suffering of those peasants who were not so fortunate.

His first work was called the *Eclogues*, a collection of ten pastoral poems. The success of this collection led Maecenas to befriend the poet and commission a more extensive work, the *Georgics*, a series of four long poems about farming. Octavian himself, by now Augustus, allegedly proposed that Virgil write his most ambitious work, an epic poem about the hero Aeneas, whose story we have encountered in previous chapters. An epic poem is a long, narrative poem in an elevated style that tells of the deeds of a legendary or real-life hero.

Virgil was another Augustan poet who helped shape much of Western literature. He authored *The Aeneid*, whose eighth book describes scenes in Roman history, among them the Battle of Actium. The poetry inspired by this naval battle helps indicate its larger and far-reaching importance.

One of the few poets to be as highly regarded as Horace, Virgil revitalized epic poetry in much the same way that his younger contemporary achieved success in lyric verse. His book *The Aeneid* was the source of poetic imitation during the lifetime of its author, and by the time of Pliny the Younger, a circle of "Virgilian poets" had already emerged. In the schools of grammar, exercises in reading, memorization, and verse composition were often based upon Virgilian examples, and by the Middle Ages, Virgil's poetry was believed to have magical qualities.

THE SHIELD OF AENEAS

In the eighth book of *The Aeneid*, the hero Aeneas receives a magnificent shield from his mother, Venus, on the eve of battle. Vulcan, god of the forge and husband of Venus (but not Aeneas's father), crafted and engraved the shield, much as he had done for Achilles in Homer's *Iliad*.

This shield, however, is not merely functional for combat. On it are scenes from Roman history—events that had already taken place by Virgil's day but were yet to come from the perspective of Aeneas. The scenes chosen for the shield had the ostensible purpose of inspiring the hero to fight to secure the future of Rome, which he both literally and symbolically would carry on his shoulders.

At the very center of the shield stands the Battle of Actium, its position suggestive of the event's importance for the history of Rome. Augustus appears, leading his people into battle and adorned with the emblems of Julius Caesar:

> there he stood
> High on the stern, and from his blessed brow
> Twin flames gushed upward, while his crest revealed
> His father's star.[54]

All the key players are present in the Virgilian scene. First,

> Agrippa,
>> Favored by winds and gods, led ships in column,
>> A towering figure, wearing on his brows
>> The coronet adorned with warships' beaks,
>> Highest distinction for command at sea.[55]

Antony is next, "with barbaric wealth / And a diversity of arms, victorious / From races of the Dawnlands." Finally, there is Cleopatra, her death by snakebite yet to come:

> The queen
>> Amidst the battle called her flotilla on
>> With a sistrum's beat, a frenzy out of Egypt,
>> Never turning her head as yet to see
>> Twin snakes of death behind.[56]

Even the gods are present at Actium, as Virgil envisions Neptune, Venus, Minerva, Mars, and above all Apollo, the god to whom Augustus would dedicate a temple after his victory.

Next, the fighting begins, but rather than concentrate on the details of battle, Virgil emphasizes Cleopatra's flight:

> The queen, appeared crying for winds to shift
> Just as she hauled up sail and slackened sheets.
> The Lord of Fire had portrayed her there,
> Amid the slaughter, pallid with death to come,
> Then borne by waves and wind from the northwest,
> While the great length of mourning Nile awaited her
> With open bays, calling the conquered home
> To his blue bosom and his hidden streams.[57]

Finally, the poet shifts to Augustus's "triple triumph" and the rejoicing throughout Rome.

Aeneas, for his part, merely wonders at the shield but understands nothing. From Virgil's readers, however, judgment is invited about the meaning of Actium, for the shield is self-consciously presented as a representation of the battle, an image constructed by Vulcan. Should we rejoice in the triumph or sympathize at all with Cleopatra? Should we focus on the restoration of order or the violence of war and the men who "raged in the fight / As from high air the dire Furies came / With Discord?"[58] These are the essential questions Virgil places before us as we watch Aeneas observe the battle for the first time.

CONCLUSIONS

Horace and Virgil deserve our attention as poets of monumental literary merit whose works achieve a sophistication and verbal refinement that cannot be fully appreciated in an English translation. From a historian's point of view, they matter less as a record of "what really happened" than as a point of entry for considering "why Actium matters."

Indeed, the Battle of Actium was rather unexciting as battles go, but it nevertheless captured the imaginations of some of Rome's greatest poets. The allure of Actium was not the military brilliance of the commanders nor the heroism of the men but rather what it meant for Rome: the beginning of the Augustan Age, with all the good and bad things such a beginning entails. If the poems can help us reevaluate the Battle of Actium with each reading, even as they appeal to us with their graceful yet powerful language and vivid imagery, then we surely owe the poets a double debt.

Approx. 1200 B.C.	Trojan War
753 B.C.	Founding of Rome
Approx. 750–700 B.C.	Homer writes *Iliad* and *Odyssey*
509 B.C.	Establishment of the Roman Republic
256 B.C.	Battle of Ecnomus
146 B.C.	Defeat of Carthage in Third Punic War
82–79 B.C.	Sulla becomes dictator
73 B.C.	Spartacus leads slave revolt
70 B.C.	Birth of Virgil
63 B.C.	Cicero becomes consul; Catilinarian Conspiracy; birth of Octavian
60 B.C.	First Triumvirate
44 B.C.	Assassination of Julius Caesar
42 B.C.	Battle of Philippi
36 B.C.	Battle of Naulochus
34 B.C.	Antony's Eastern triumph; "Donations of Alexandria"
32 B.C.	Antony at Actium
31 B.C.	Battle of Actium
30 B.C.	Suicides of Antony and Cleopatra
29 B.C.	Octavian returns to Rome
27 B.C.	Octavian becomes "Augustus"
23 B.C.	Death of Marcellus; conspiracy against Augustus; publication of Horace's *Odes*
19 B.C.	Death of Virgil
16–13 B.C.	Augustus in Gaul
9 B.C.	Dedication of the *Ara Pacis*
A.D. 4	Augustus adopts Tiberius
A.D. 14	Death of Augustus

Achilles, 14
Actium, Battle of
  and Agrippa aiding
    Octavian, 69, 70, 71,
    72, 74, 75, 76, 77
  Antony's approach to,
    70
  Antony's defeat in, 11,
    70-72, 76-77
  and Antony's escape to
    Egypt, 76-77
  Antony's first move in,
    76
  Antony's motives in,
    72
  Antony's position in,
    71, 74-75
  Antony's ships in, 70,
    74, 76
  Antony's skill in, 69
  Antony's strategy for,
    70, 74-75, 76
  and approach to
    Actium, 69-70
  beginning of, 75-76
  and Cleopatra's escape
    to Egypt, 76-77
  Cleopatra's ships in,
    11, 74, 76, 77
  date of, 11, 73
  end of, 77
  fighting in, 72-77
  final preparations for,
    69-72
  initial skirmishes in,
    70-71
  in literature, 99-103,
    105-107
  and mythic beginnings
    of Rome, 12-14
  and Octavian meeting
    "Good Fortune"
    and "Victory," 73
  Octavian's approach to,
    70, 71

and Octavian's negative
    view of Antony and
    Cleopatra, 57
  Octavian's position in,
    71, 74
  Octavian's return to
    Rome after, 79, 87-
    88
  Octavian's ships in,
    66-67, 70, 73-74
  Octavian's strategy in,
    76
  Octavian's victory in,
    11-12, 77
aedile, 17
Aemulius, 14-15
Aeneas, and *Aeneid,* 14,
    93-94, 103, 105-107
Aeneid (Virgil), 14, 93-94,
    103, 105-107
Africa, 27, 37, 57, 58
  See also Egypt
Agamemnon, 13
Agrippa, Marcus
  and Battle of Actium,
    69, 70, 71, 72, 74, 75,
    76, 77
  on foreign missions, 91
  and Julia, 89-90, 94
  in literature, 106
  and navy, 47-49, 67
  and Sextus Pompeius,
    48, 49-51, 53
Ahenobarbus, Cnaeus
  Domitius, 58-59
Ahenobarbus, Lucius
  Domitius, 24
Alba Longa, 14
Alban kings, 14
Alexandria, Antony and
  Cleopatra's escape to,
    76-77
  See also Egypt
Ambracian Gulf, 11, 69,
    71

Anchises, 14
Antiochus, 65
Antony, Marc
  and Africa, 58
  and Armenia, 56
  and Battle of Philippi,
    40-43
  and Brutus and
    Cassius, 32, 33, 34,
    39-43
  and Caesar's funeral,
    32
  in charge of Rome
    after Caesar's death,
    31-36
  in charge of Rome in
    Caesar's absence, 27
  children of, 82, 84
  and Cicero, 34-36
  and Cleopatra, 46, 56,
    57, 59-61, 78-82, 84
  and control of East,
    55
  as Dionysus, 80
  and escape to Egypt
    after Battle of
    Actium, 76-77
  and Gaul, 33, 37, 58
  and Greek associations,
    14
  in literature, 32, 101,
    106
  and Macedonia, 33
  and Octavia as wife,
    59-60
  and Octavian, 33, 35-36,
    43, 55-61, 78, 79-80,
    83, 84. *See also*
    Actium, Battle of
  Octavian's attack on in
    Egypt, 79-80, 84
  and Parthia, 55-56
  and Sardinia, 58
  and Second Triumvi-
    rate, 36-37, 58

and Senate, 58-59, 60
and Sextus Pompeius,
    32-33, 49, 53
and Sicily, 58
and Spain, 58
suicide of, 80-82
will of, 60-61
See also Actium, Battle
    of
Antyllus, 82, 84
Aphrodite, 13, 14
Apollophanes, 49-50
Appian, 43, 53
aqueducts, 18, 92-93
Ara Pacis Augustae
    ("Augustus's Altar of
    Peace"), 91
Armenian Campaign, 56
army
    Octavian disbanding,
        88
    of Roman Republic,
        18
Arruntius, 74, 76
Artavasdes, 56
"Art of Poetry, The"
    (Horace), 100
Ascanius, 14
asp, and Cleopatra's
    suicide, 83
Athena, 13
Atia, 20
Atticus, 34
Augustus, 89-97
    and *Aeneid*, 14, 93-94,
        103, 105-107
    Age of, 14, 89-97, 99-
        103, 105-107
    and cash disburse-
        ments, 95-96
    and conspiracy to
        restore republic, 90
    and daughter, 89-90,
        92, 94
    death of, 94-96

and domestic programs,
    91-93, 96-97
as financial manager,
    92
and Gaul, 91
as god, 94
legacy of, 96-97
and legal measures, 92
and literature, 14, 93-
    94, 99-103, 105-107
and Marcellus, 89, 94
Octavian as, 89
and Parthians, 90-91
power of, 90
and public buildings,
    92-93
and resignation of
    consulship, 90
and Senate, 90, 94
and succession, 89, 94
will of, 95-96
See also Octavian
Augustus of Prima Porta
    (sculpture), 91

bath houses, 93
Bellona, Temple of, 61
bridges, 18, 92-93
Bronze Age, 12-14
Brundisium, 24
Brutus, Decimus, 36
Brutus, Marcus Junius
    amnesty to, 32, 33, 34,
        36
    and Antony, 32, 33,
        34
    and assassination of
        Caesar, 28-29
    and Cicero, 34
    defeat of at Battle of
        Philippi, 39-43
    and Macedonia, 36
    and Octavian, 36, 37,
        39-43
    and Senate, 36

Caepio, Fannius, 90
Caesar, Gaius, 94
Caesar, Gaius Julius
    and Africa, 27
    and Asia Minor, 27
    assassination of, 28-29,
        46
    and Caesarians vs.
        republicans, 31-32
    and civil war, 23-24, 26
    and Cleopatra, 27, 83,
        84
    as consul, 21-22, 26-27
    and daughter, 21, 23
    as descendant of
        Aeneas and
        Aphrodite, 14
    as dictator, 26, 27-28
    and Egypt, 26, 27
    and First Triumvirate,
        20-24, 26-28, 37
    and Gallic campaign,
        22, 23, 24
    as god, 39-40
    in literature, 28, 29, 32
    and navy, 66
    and Octavian as great-
        nephew, 11, 14
    and Octavian as heir,
        32, 33, 36, 39
    and Pompey, 21, 23-24,
        26, 29, 37
    and refusal to be
        crowned king, 28
    and Roman calendar,
        27
    and Senate, 20, 21, 23,
        32, 33, 39
    son of, 82-83, 84
    and state funeral, 32
Caesarians, 31-32
Caesarion, 82-83, 84
calendar, and Caesar, 27
"calling out," 79-80
Calpurnia, 29

Calvisius, 47
Campus Martius, 91, 94
Canidius, 55
Carrhae, 23
Carthage, 63-66, 80
Cassius. *See* Longinus,
    Gaius Cassius
catapults, 48
Catilina, Lucius Sergius
    ("Catiline"), 19-20, 34
Cato, 23
census, 88
Cicero, Marcus Tullius
    and Antony, 34-36
    and Brutus and Cassius,
        34
    and Catilinian Con-
        spiracy, 19-20, 34
    and Clodius, 22-23
    and First Triumvirate,
        21
    and Pompey, 26
Cleopatra, 27
    and Antony, 46, 56, 57,
        59-61, 78-82, 84
    and Antony's suicide,
        80-82
    and Caesar, 27, 83, 84
    and Caesarion, 82-83, 84
    children of, 82-83, 84
    and escape to Egypt
        after Battle of
        Actium, 76-77, 106
    in literature, 100, 102-
        103, 106, 107
    and Octavian, 56-61, 79,
        82-84, 88. *See also*
        Actium, Battle of
    Octavian's attack on in
        Egypt, 79, 82-83
    and Senate, 61
    suicide of, 80-81, 83-84,
        100, 102-103
    See also Actium, Battle
        of

"Cleopatra Ode"
    (Horace), 102-103
client kingdoms, 55
Clodius, 22-23
Consilium Plebis, 17-18
conspirators. *See* Brutus,
    Marcus Junius; Longi-
    nus, Gaius Cassius
consuls, 16-17, 19-20, 23
Corcyra, 70
Cornificus, 47, 49
corn shortages, 46-47
Corsica, 46
Crassus, Canidius, 59
Crassus, Marcus Licinius,
    19
    death of, 23
    and First Triumvirate,
        20-23, 37
    and Senate, 20, 21, 23
Cumae, Battle of, 47
Cursus honorum ("honors
    race"), 16-17, 18

De Bello Civile (*On the
    Civil War*)/*Pharsalia*
    (Lucan), 26
Demochares, 49
dictator, 33
Dio, Cassius, 69, 72, 76
Discord, goddess of, 13
Divus Julius, 39
Dolabella, 33
Domitius, Gnaeus, 71
Donations of Alexandria,
    56
Drusilla, Livia, 47
Drusus, 94
Dyrrhachium, 26

Eastern triumph, 56
Eclogues (Virgil), 103
Ecnomus, Battle of, 65
education, in Roman
    Republic, 16

Egypt
    and Antony and
        Cleopatra's escape
        from Battle of
        Actium to, 77, 78,
        106
    and Caesar, 27
    conspirators in, 82
    Octavian fighting
        against Antony and
        Cleopatra in, 79-80,
        82-85
    Pompey executed in,
        26
    See also Cleopatra
Epirus, 64
Epistles (Horace), 100
Epodes (Horace), 100,
    101-102
equites (equestrians), 18,
    19
Eros, 81
Etna, Mount, 51

First Triumvirate, 20-24,
    26-28, 37
Flaccus, Quintus Horatius.
    See Horace
Forum, 92
Forum Gallorum, battles
    at, 36

Gallus, Gaius Cornelius,
    79, 85
Gaul, 63
    and Antony, 33, 37, 58
    and Augustus, 91
    and Gallic Wars, 22,
        23, 24
    imperial mint in, 92
    and Lepidus, 37
Georgics (Virgil), 103
Golden Age, in Greco-
    Roman mythology, 12,
    14

golden apple, and mythic
    beginnings of Rome,
    13
grain shortages, 46-47
grappling hook, 51
Greece, 13-14, 24

Harpax, 48
Hector, 14
Helen, 13-14
Hera, 13
Hiera, 49
Hiero, 64
Hirtius, 35-36
Horace, 93, 99, 100-103,
    107
horse, and Trojan War,
    13-14

Ides of March, 28-29
Illyricum, 57, 87
imperium, of Augustus, 90
Insteius, 74

Janus, Temple of, 88
javelins, 67
Julia (Augustus's daughter),
    89-90, 92, 94
Julia (Caesar's daughter),
    21, 23

Latifundia, 18
Leges Juliae ("Julian
    Laws"), 92
Lepidus, Marcus Aemilius
    as consul, 37
    as *Magister Equitum,*
        31
    as *Pontifex Maximus,* 32
    and Second Triumvi-
        rate, 36-37
    and Sextus Pompeius,
        49, 53
    and Spain, 37
"Letter to the Pisones"

(Horace), 100
Leucas, 71
Lex Campana, 21
libraries, 93
literature, in Augustan
    Age, 14, 93-94
    and Battle of Actium,
        99-103, 105-107
Livia, 94
Livy, 93
Longinus, Gaius Cassius
    ("Cassius")
    amnesty to, 32, 33, 34,
        36
    and Antony, 32, 33, 34
    and assassination of
        Caesar, 28-29
    and Cicero, 34
    defeat of at Battle of
        Philippi, 39-41, 42,
        43
    and Octavian, 36, 37,
        39-43
    and Senate, 36
    and Syria, 36
Lucan, 26
Lurius, 74, 76

Macedonia, 33, 36
Macedonian Wars, 65
Macrobius, 80
Maecenas, 93, 99, 100,
    101, 103
Magister Equitum
    ("Master of the
    Horse"), 27, 31
magistrates, 16
Mamertines, 64
Marcellus, 24, 89, 94
Marius, Gaius, 18
Maro, Publius Vergilius.
    See Virgil
Mars, 15, 92
Menas, 47
Menecrates, 47

Menelaus, 13
Messana, 53, 64
Messina, Straits of, 46
Methone, 70
Mikalitzi, 70
Mithradates, king of
    Pontus, 19
    son of, 27
Musa, Antonius, 89
Myconium, Mount, 51
Mylae, Battle of, 49-50
mythology, and beginnings
    of Rome, 12-16

Naulochus, Battle of, 51-
    53, 101
navy
    history of, 47-49, 63-66,
        67
    and Roman naval
        warfare, 47-53, 63-
        67. *See also* Actium,
        Battle of
Nero, Tiberius Claudius,
    94
Numitor, 14-15

Octavia, 59-60
Octavian
    and Africa, 37, 57
    and Antony, 33, 35-36,
        43, 55-61, 78, 79-80,
        83, 84. *See also*
        Actium, Battle of
    and Armenian Cam-
        paign, 56
    and Battle of Philippi,
        40-43
    birth of, 20
    and Brutus and Cassius,
        36, 37, 39-43
    as Caesar's heir, 32, 33,
        36, 39
    and census, 88
    and Cleopatra, 56-61,

79, 82-84, 88
and closing Temple of
 Janus, 88
and conspirators in
 Egypt, 82
as consul, 36
as descendant of
 Aeneas and
 Aphrodite, 14
and disbanding army,
 88
and divorce from
 Scribonia, 47
in Egypt fighting
 against Antony and
 Cleopatra, 79-80,
 82-85
and end of Roman
 civil wars, 12, 85
and evocation of
 Egypt's gods before
 attack, 79-80
and Gaius Julius Caesar
 Octavianus as
 name, 33
as great-nephew of
 Caesar, 11, 14
and Illyricum, 57, 87
and marriage to Livia
 Drusilla, 47
and navy, 47-49, 67
and *Pax Romana*, 12,
 91
as *Princeps Senatus,*
 88
and public works, 57-
 58
and return to Rome
 after Battle of
 Actium, 79, 87-88
as Rome's first
 emperor, 89
and Sardinia, 37, 47
and Second Triumvi-
 rate, 36-37

and Senate, 59, 88-89,
 90
and Sextus Pompeius,
 47-53, 101
and Sicily, 37
and Spain, 57
See also Actium, Battle
 of; Augustus
Octavianus, Gaius Julius
 Caesar, 33
 See also Octavian
Octavius, Gaius. *See*
 Octavian
Octavius, Marcus, 74
Odes (Horace), 100
Odysseus, 13
Ovid, 93

Palatine Hill, 15
Pansa, 35-36
Paris, 13
Parthia/Parthians, 23,
 55-56, 90-91
Paterculus, Velleius, 41
Patrae, 70, 71
patricians, 17, 18
Pax Romana, 12, 91
Pedius, Quintus, 36
Pharsalus, 26, 29
Philippi, Battle of, 39-43
Phraates, 56
pirates, 19, 46
Plancus, 60
plebeians, 17-18
plumbing, 93
Plutarch, 32, 59, 77, 80-
 81, 83-84
Polybius, 65
Pompeius, Sextus, 32-33,
 36, 45-53, 101
Pompey the Great
 and Caesar, 21, 23-24,
 26, 29, 37
 and civil war, 23-24,
 26

and execution of in
 Egypt, 26
and First Triumvirate,
 20-24, 26-27, 37
and marriage to Julia
 (Caesar's daughter),
 21, 23
and pirates, 19
and Senate, 20, 23
and son. *See* Pompeius,
 Sextus
Pontifex Maximus ("Chief
 Priest"), 32
Pontus, 19, 27
Portus Julius, 48, 49
praetors, 17
Princeps Senatus, Octavian
 as, 88
Proculeius, 83
Ptolemy, 26
Ptolemy XIII, 27
Publicola, 74, 76
Punic Wars, 63-66, 80
Pyrrhus, 64

quaestors, 16
quinqueremes, 65

Remus, 15
republicans, 31-32, 90
 and Battle of Philippi,
 39-43
*Res Gestae (Book of
 Accomplishments)*
 (Octavian), 43
Rhea Silvia, 14, 15
roads, 18, 92-93
Roman Republic, 16-20
 and assassination of
 Julius Caesar, 28-29,
 46
 and Battle of Philippi,
 39-43
 end of, 11-12, 20
 establishment of, 11

and First Triumvirate, 20-24, 26-28, 37, 58
government of, 16-17
internal conflicts in, 17-21
and naval warfare, 47-53, 63-67. *See also* Actium, Battle of
and Octavian versus Antony and Cleopatra, 55-61. *See also* Actium, Battle of
and Second Triumvirate, 31-37
Senate in, 16, 17, 18-19, 20, 21, 23
and Sextus Pompeius, 45-53

Rome
founding of, 11
kings as rulers of, 16
mythic beginnings of, 12-16
and Trojan War, 13-14
See also Roman Republic
Romulus, 15
Rubicon River, 24

Salvidienus, 46
Sardinia, 37, 46, 47, 58
Satires (Horace), 100

Scribonia, 47
Second Punic War, 65
Second Triumvirate, 31-37, 39-43, 45-53, 58
Senate
and Antony, 58-59, 60
and Augustus, 90, 94
and Caesar, 32, 33, 39
and Carthaginians, 64
and Catilina, 19-20
and Cleopatra, 61
and First Triumvirate, 21
and navy, 64-65
and Octavian, 59, 88-89
in Roman Republic, 16, 17, 18-19, 20, 21, 23
and Rome's money supply, 92
and Second Triumvirate, 37
sewage, 93
Shakespeare, William, 28, 29, 32, 80, 81-82
she-wolf, 15
Sicily, 37, 46, 49-53, 58, 64
Sinon, 13-14
slaves, 18, 48
Sosius, Gaius, 55, 58-59, 71, 74, 76
Spain, 20, 24, 32-33, 37, 57, 58
Spartacus, 19

Strongyle, 49
Suetonius, 42
Sulla, Lucius Cornelius, 18-19, 24
Syracuse, 64
Syria, 23, 33, 36

Tarquin the Proud, 16
Tauromenium, 49
Taurus, Statilius, 49, 71
Tenedos, 13, 14
theaters, and Augustus, 93
Tiberius, 94
Tiber River, 15
Tisenus, 51
Titius, Marcus, 53, 60, 71
Tribunes of the People, 17-18, 19
Tribunician Power, and Augustus, 90
triremes, 65, 67
Trojan War, 13-14
Tyndaris, 50

"Veni, Vidi, Vici (I came, I saw, I conquered)", 27
Ventidius, 55
Vesta, priestesses of, 14
Vestal Virgins, 60
Virgil, 14, 89, 93-94, 103, 105-107

page:

10: Library of Congress, LC-US262-115873
15: © Alexander Burkatowski/
    CORBIS
22: Hierophont Collection
25: © Bettmann/CORBIS
30: © Bettmann/CORBIS
35: © Archivo Iconografico, S.A./
    CORBIS
38: © Giraudon/Art Resource, NY
43: © Hulton/Archive, Getty Images
44: © Timothy McCarthy/
    Art Resource, NY
48: © Archivo Iconografico, S.A./
    CORBIS
52: © Araldo de Luca/CORBIS

54: © Scala/Art Resource, NY
60: © Bettmann/CORBIS
62: © Clore Collection, Tate Gallery,
    London, Art Resource, NY
66: © Christel Gerstenberg/CORBIS
68: © North Carolina Museum of Art/
    CORBIS
75: © Bettmann/CORBIS
78: Library of Congress
84: © Hulton/Archive, Getty Images
86: © Erich Lessing/Art Resource, NY
91: ©Bettmann/CORBIS
95: © Vanni Archive/CORBIS
98: © Scala/Art Resource, NY
104: © Massimo Listri/CORBIS

Cover: © Bettmann/CORBIS
Frontis: 21st Century Publishing

David J. Califf received his Ph.D. from the University of Wisconsin–Madison and currently teaches Latin and English literature at The Academy of Notre Dame in Villanova, Pennsylvania. A published Latin poet, he is the author of *A Guide to Latin Meter and Verse Composition*, the *Marathon* volume of the "Great Battles" series, and articles on classical poetry and ancient Greek literary criticism. As a hobby, he gives college tours at New York's Metropolitan Museum of Art in conjunction with Kean University.

Caspar W. Weinberger was the fifteenth secretary of defense, serving under President Ronald Reagan from 1981 to 1987. Born in California in 1917, he fought in the Pacific during World War II then went on to pursue a law career. He became an active member of the California Republican Party and was named the party's chairman in 1962. Over the next decade, Weinberger held several federal government offices, including chairman of the Federal Trade Commission and secretary of health, education, and welfare. Ronald Reagan appointed him to be secretary of defense in 1981. He became one of the most respected secretaries of defense in history and served longer than any previous secretary except for Robert McNamara (who served 1961–1968). Today, Weinberger is chairman of the influential *Forbes* magazine.